CHOW!

"CHOW!"

*Secrets of Chinese Cooking
With Selected Recipes
by Dolly Chow
(Mrs. C. T. Wang)*

*Illustrated by
Henry Liu*

CHARLES E. TUTTLE COMPANY
RUTLAND, VERMONT & TOKYO, JAPAN

Representatives
Continental Europe: BOXERBOOKS, INC., *Zurich*
British Isles: PRENTICE-HALL INTERNATIONAL, INC., *London*
Australasia: PAUL FLESCH & CO., PTY. LTD., *Melbourne*
Canada: HURTIG PUBLISHERS, *Edmonton*

Published by the Charles E. Tuttle Company, Inc.
of Rutland, Vermont & Tokyo, Japan
with editorial offices at Suido 1-chome, 2-6
Bunkyo-ku, Tokyo, Japan

International Standard Book No. 0-8048-1073-7

First edition, 1952
Twelfth printing, 1974

CONTENTS

INTRODUCTION

Of all human frailties that of the gourmet is probably the gentlest and the most amiable. His very weakness marks him out as that rare thing, a man of taste and discernment. It can do no harm to anyone but himself and need not harm even him if he has wisdom as well.

To all gourmets I commend this book. If, in these unhappy times, they cannot come to China to see and eat for themselves, this book will build for them an easy and a pretty bridge by which, from their own homes, they can reach the simple and surprising delights of Chinese cooking.

In the matter of food, as in all else that has grace, the Chinese have long been past-masters. They put into the cooking of it all the loving care for detail, the daintiness, the spice and the

wit that characterise their art and their under-
standing of the business of life, which is one
of the chiefest of their charms.   In China every
province boasts its own fashion of preparing food
and claims that it is the best.   When you eat
you tend to admit the claim without demur.
But a practised palate will tell in a twinkling
whether the juiciness of a duck or the crispness
of the crackling of a suckling pig is due to the
craft of Cantonese, Pekinese, Szechuanese, or
what you will.   For myself, I cannot pretend
to so much *"expertise"*.   Nor does this book set
out to guide you to it or to cover the vast
field of Chinese cooking.   It offers seventy-five
straightforward recipes of every day, but none
the less delicious, food which is within the reach
of everyone, which calls for no expense and
which will quench the passions of the greedy
and enchant the finer feelings of the gourmet
alike.

The authoress, Dolly Chow, is the daughter
of Sir Shouson Chow, a well-known and much

respected member of the Chinese community of Hongkong.   She has been so kind as to give me some lessons in cooking at which I had the emotion both of finding out the secrets of the Chinese kitchen and of eating the dishes as they came off the fire.   If you had seen and tasted what I did, you would agree with me that no one is better fitted than Dolly Chow to introduce you to the dressing of Chinese food.

Maria Teresa Clark Kerr

PREFACE

The Chinese long ago developed a way of life which has found some favour among visitors to China. The earliest records show that Chinese of the remotest antiquity not only enjoyed the chase; they also had good methods of dealing with the fruits it yielded.

The histories do not state clearly when traditional Chinese cookery methods became fixed, but they do record, in prose and verse, the ecstasies of those men of fine discernment and taste who knew that men ate not merely in order to live. Dr. Johnson's well-known observation that he could always smell a good dinner may readily find its echo from many Chinese scholars. However, only by a long process of empirical trial and error were those subtle flavours discovered which have made men long exiled from home write wistfully of the province which gave rise to a lordly dish.

The author of the book does not attempt to compete with men like Su Tung-po or Yuan

Mei, whose writings on the art of cooking have become a classic. Her aim is much more modest and her methods are much more practical. She would tell you how, with the minimum of materials and trouble, you may prepare food as the Chinese do; she would demonstrate that it is worth while taking a little time to learn the art; and the results are so much more satisfactory. Those who have had the privilege of tasting a meal prepared by her will suspect magic—but the secret is here. If the garden of good Chinese food is an enchanted land (as many aver that it is) then the author is a good guide.

F. T. CHENG
Chinese Ambassador in London

FOREWORD

Modes of travel have so improved in recent years that the world seems to have really grown so much smaller and international intercourse has become so much easier. Increasing numbers of visitors are coming to China each year and they sooner or later become acquainted with Chinese food. It is natural that many of these people find themselves desirous of learning something of the mysteries of Chinese cooking and the art of imparting the subtle flavourings to the various dishes. There can be no doubt that the taste for Chinese food among foreigners is growing very considerably. The introduction of Chinese food at the well-known hotels in Hongkong and the increasing popularity of Chinese restaurants in Shanghai testify to the increasing interest of foreigners in Chinese cooking.

Although East and West are getting closer through increased contact, Chinese customs still differ widely from those of the West and, in some instances, are actually the reverse of Western ideas. To avoid misunderstandings as well as to assist in the full appreciation of Chinese food in the surroundings of Chinese homes and restaurants some knowledge of these customs will be found very helpful:

At a Chinese dinner the host sits opposite the guest of honour because, from the oriental point of view, the highest seat should logically be opposite the lowest. The left-hand side of the host is regarded as being higher than the right-hand side. It is permissible by Chinese custom to remove the short outer jacket, wearing only a long robe for dining. Soup and fish are served only at the end of the dinner instead of at the beginning as is the custom of the West. Warm wine is provided, in contrast to the Western custom of icy cold drinks.

The interior surroundings, in the way of furniture and decorations, are usually very plain in most of the old-style restaurants.

At a Chinese meal such articles as milk, bread, butter, or cheese are never served. Sometimes dishes considered by us to be rare and delicious may be thought unpalatable for consumption by foreigners—as, for example, bears' paws, chicken feet, ducks' tongues, pigs' trotters, etc.

It is not surprising, then, that a stranger confronted for the first time with unaccustomed articles of our diet should feel dismayed and uncomfortable. As an illustration, I recall the experience of a friend of mine, an English lady of title, who was on her first visit to this country to see her son, the head of a large foreign tobacco company in Peiping. Her first encounter with Chinese food was at a dinner in a restaurant. The unaccustomed dishes upset her so badly that she practically decided not to accept any further invitations to Chinese dinners. This was the excuse she made to me when I asked her later to dinner. However, she finally persuaded herself to try once again, and accepted my invitation. Her second adventure was more fortunate, and she told me that on this occasion she found the food really delicious and was now anxious to make a third trial. From that time onwards my friend would eat and enjoy herself even in restaurants. She returned to England many years ago. In one of her letters to me she reminds me of the delicious dishes she had tasted while in China. Had this lady not remained long enough to have had the opportunity of discovering really attractive dishes, she most likely would have concluded that Chinese food was revolting, and would have conveyed this impression to the people back in her own country.

Many of my foreign friends have expressed the desire to see, in a handy form, an explanation of Chinese customs and practices supplementing the information on the preparation and enjoyment of Chinese food, and have thus given me encouragement and confidence to attempt the task in this little book. I also desire to assist my friends to prepare a few dishes in their own homes so that they may be able to demonstrate how delicious Chinese food really is.

It is my sincere hope that this little volume will be helpful to all epicures who desire pleasure and enjoyment from the exotic as well as the delicious in food.

D. C.

THE HOUSEWIFE AND COOKING

One of the duties of a good housewife is to appreciate the importance of cooking and its close relation to domestic happiness. This opinion prevailed even in the days of Confucius. We learn from the Classics that Confucius was particularly fastidious as regards food for we are told that:—

1. He refused to partake of wine and dried meat bought in the market.
2. He refused to eat meat which was not cut properly nor what was served without the correct sauce.
3. He refused to eat anything badly cooked or not in season.
4. He liked his rice polished white and his meat minced finely.

Had there been such conveniences as are now available—the equipment of a modern kitchen—and had there been properly conducted schools of cookery where the necessary knowledge might be acquired, Chinese house-

1

wives in ancient times would have been able to maintain satisfactorily a high standard of culinary art in their households. The modern housewife is more fortunately situated. She can employ a good cook and supervise his work, thus doing away with the necessity of purchasing food from outside herself. She can procure a mincing machine to mince meat to any desired fineness; she can buy perfectly white machine-milled rice and she can easily procure any sauce to suit any taste thanks to the skill and experience of modern organisations. In fact she has everything in her favour these days; all she has to do is to learn how to cook.

One would expect then that there should be less friction in modern households. Unfortunately this is not so. Perhaps it is that Confucius, being wise, was exacting only in the matter of food, while modern husbands are fastidious and troublesome in other directions as well. However, experience tells us that, by eliminating one cause of domestic disturbance—the food question—the modern housewife has gone far towards securing domestic peace.

"Good appetite brings happiness" 食得是福 is an old saying worthy of the housewife's attention. To stimulate the appetite is the one object of our culinary art, the knowledge of which enables the housewife to produce dishes so deliciously flavoured and so attractively served, that they would tempt even the most fastidious husband. The same knowledge will also help her to bring the changes in the diet which, like a change of air, can only be beneficial to the appetite and health.

To the conscientious housewife then, who is solicitous of domestic peace and happiness, the science and art of cooking should have a definite appeal. The servant problem fortunately is not so acute in this country; so the housewife, once she has acquired proficiency in the art of cooking, needs to have less uneasiness of mind in regard to the menial work of the kitchen. Her part will merely consist of direction and supervision, if necessary. The Chinese say, with truth, that just as those who live near water know the nature of fishes, and those near mountains learn the melody of birds, so those who remain close to the kitchen acquire the knowledge of good food. 近水知魚性，近山識鳥音，近厨得佳食．

GOOD APPETITE BRINGS HAPPINESS

THE ART OF COOKING

China is a country where the appreciation of good food is developed into a fine art. Chinese are epicures. Their cooking is distinctive: No other cooking resembles it in any way.

Chinese food is rich, but not greasy: it is delicately flavoured, but not pungently spicy. Cook what is freshly slaughtered, and eat what is freshly cooked 現殺現烹現熟現食 is a doctrine universally recognised throughout China. It is better that one should wait for the meal than that the meal should wait for one. Variety is another important feature. A Chinese dish almost always consists of a mixture of food-stuffs—the meat or fish is generally cooked with, and improved by, the addition of some appropriate vegetable. All the material to be used is cut into convenient size in the kitchen before serving, so that no carving instruments are required at table. All the condiments are added during the process of cooking, thus doing away with the necessity of the usual cruet. The only

exception is some soya bean sauce provided at
the table in case it is required.

With the passage of time the methods of
cooking have necessarily undergone many improvements as compared with the original crude
processes. Expert cooks in different parts of
China have introduced numerous improvements,
and, with China being such a vast country, its
component parts differing widely not only in
climate and customs, but even in the spoken
language, it is only to be expected that different
terms are found in different localities for the
same way of cooking. For instance, roasting
in the North is known as *K'ao* 烤 while in the
South it is called *Shao* 燒. Similarly *Shao Fan*
燒飯 in North China means cooking rice, but
in Canton they say *Chu Fan* 煮飯. In these
circumstances I have to employ those terms
which are more commonly used and are more
generally understood. All the terms used in
this little book are in the National language,
that is, Mandarin (*Kuo Yu* 國語).

Methods of cooking.

1. *Shao K'ao* 燒烤 *means Roasting*

There are two different ways of doing this:

one is roasting over an open fire known as *Ming Lu* 明爐, while the other is roasting in an oven *K'ao Lu* 烤爐.

By the first mentioned method we prepare roast suckling pig and barbecued Peking duck. In exactly the same way the Russians make "shaslick" and the Javanese "sateh" dishes, which are well known to foreigners in the Orient. The Cantonese dish known as "gold coin chicken" consisting of a combination of alternate pieces of ham, chicken and pork is made the same way. Material for barbecuing should be hung for six to seven hours, and then covered with the proper condiments. Then it is fixed to a metal fork or skewer and held over a strong charcoal fire. Constant turning of the fork is necessary to ensure even roasting. In barbecuing a whole pig the skin should be punctured before roasting to secure an even surface at the end of the operation. A Chinese oven is usually built of brick and clay, with two openings, one below and one above in the form of a very short chimney. A charcoal fire is started inside: after half an hour when the oven is sufficiently hot, the fire is damped down by placing a thin metal sheet over the charcoal.

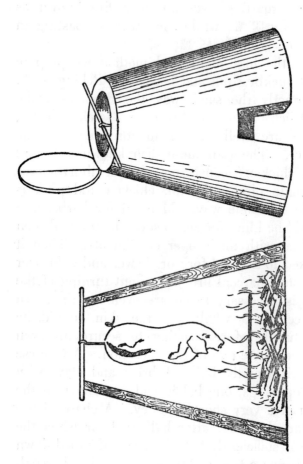

(A CHINESE OVEN)

The material to be roasted is hung inside the oven, and both openings are closed. The result is identical with that of a modern gas or electric oven.

2. *Cheng* 蒸 *means Steaming.*

This is a simple and economical process of cooking with steam rising from boiling water. By this method the nutritive juice and flavour of the material are conserved. It is specially recommended for preparing fish. In the home, steaming is very often carried out by utilising the steam from boiling rice. At other times it is done by means of a special cooker made of split bamboo called *Cheng Lung* 蒸籠 meaning a steam cage. In steaming *Chiao Tzu* 餃子 or dumplings, these are placed directly on a piece of damp cloth spread over the cage instead of on China plates. This method of cooking is frequently used at home, but not often in restaurants.

3. *Ch'ao* 炒 *means Frying with a little fat over a quick fire. Frequent quick turning is essential.*

Most of the expensive dishes are prepared by this way of cooking. The important point in this process is the high temperature employed, which ensures quick cooking. If the temperature is not sufficiently high, the meat will not be tender. On this account it is not advisable to fry more than a pound of meat at a time: if more is needed the process should be repeated several times. When more than one ingredient has to be dealt with, they should be first fried separately and then mixed together, the meat being left to the last always. The Chinese frying-pan being convex, and not flat bottomed, the turning is more conveniently done.

4. *Chien* 煎 *Sautéing or Frying with a small quantity of fat over a gentle fire. Turning is necessary only when the meat has sufficiently browned.*

This process is also applied as a preliminary treatment to poultry and meat before stewing or boiling, for two reasons. Firstly, it makes the meat more palatable. Secondly, it tends to eliminate any excessive "muttony" or "fishy" flavour.

5. *Cha* 炸 *means Frying in deep fat at a high temperature.*

The substance to be cooked by this process is immersed in boiling oil. Sometimes the meat is covered with a coating of flour before it is dropped into the oil, to prevent toughening or overcooking. Meat treated by this process is very indigestible, though it is very tasty, so it is not advisable to employ this method too frequently at home.

6. *Men* 爓 *means Stewing.*

By this method the meat and vegetables are cooked together with a small quantity of water at a moderate temperature for a long time. The juices of the meat and vegetables are retained in the liquid and the long and slow process of cooking renders the material both tender and delicious.

7. *Tun* 燉 *means cooking by use of a double boiler.*

The material for cooking is contained in a covered vessel like a casserole-dish placed in a pan of boiling water. Meat so treated is more palatable than by simply boiling. More water is required than in stewing, otherwise the process is much the same. This is the best way of making soup, when special care should be exercised to seal down the cover with wet tissue paper. In winter this process is very popular.

8. *Ao* 熬 *means Simmering.*

This is a simple process of boiling very

slowly.   Care must be taken to avoid too rapid
evaporating, and not to uncover the pot too
often.   The simmering process must be continued without interruption until the time of
serving.   It is also termed *Po* 煲.

FLAVOURING.

Various flavouring agents are employed, the
most common being onions 葱, ginger 薑, and
garlic 蒜頭.   Reference to the ancient writings
seems to show that they are made to serve a
double purpose, for, apart from imparting a
distinct flavour to the food, some of them are
believed to have medicinal qualities as well.
For instance, the onion, which forms a constant
ingredient in the preparation of fish, is supposed
to be able to counteract any possible fish-poison-
ing, while ginger is reputed to have stimulating
properties.   Garlic and bean relish 豆豉 form
an excellent flavouring for fish or pork.   Red
pepper and star aniseed 花椒八角 go well with
beef and duck.   The usual method employed
for the addition of flavouring is as follows:—
Heat a little lard in a frying pan, then add the
flavouring agent, only a small quantity being
used—a slice of ginger or a clove of garlic.

Fry until a light brown. The material to be cooked is now added and the cooking is continued as planned.

USE OF FLOUR.

The use of flour when shaping meat balls or thickening gravy is termed *Ch'ien* 縴. Sometimes a coating of flour is added to meat destined for frying to prevent it from being too easily overdone. Paper has been known to replace flour for the same purpose. Bean flour 豆 粉 or caltrop flour 菱 粉 are commonly employed by Chinese. Corn flour (corn starch) is equally good for this purpose.

SELECTION OF INGREDIENTS

The quality of the ingredients plays an important part in good cooking. Just as no good painter can work well with a broken brush or dried up paints, so no good cook can succeed without the correct kind of ingredients. For instance, in choosing chickens, poulets are more desirable because their meat is more tender; on the other hand, with duck the male species is preferable. For stewing, steaming, and the Chinese way of frying, use spring chickens; for roasting choose capons, while for making chicken soup, when the meat will not be served, old birds may be used. Fillet should be used for frying, flank for making meat balls, and loin for roasting. Eat everything in season, and you will get more palatable and more economical dishes. *Sam Lai* 三 黎 or *Shih Yu* 時 魚 (i.e. shad) is, as its name implies, a season fish, and when in season is in great demand. The fish swims up the Yangtsze and other rivers to spawn. On the return journey, its eyes become reddish in colour and it is not as fat as when it started. For this reason red-eyed *Sam Lai* is considered inferior in quality and can be obtained at cheaper prices.

In the case of vegetables the "heart" only should be used for cooking. Bamboo shoots and mushrooms can be prepared with or without meat. They are equally delicious either way.

SERVING

The appearance of the food when served is another important factor which should not be overlooked. Well-arranged dishes attract the eye and when a pleasant flavour accompanies them, the appetite cannot but be stimulated.

Plain Daily Meal

This is a general rule: it applies to all forms of cooking, Chinese and foreign alike. Vegetarians fully recognise its importance: they have giblets, roast duck, boiled chicken and other dishes, all of them being prepared with bean curd "skins". The dishes are so cleverly made that they look exactly like the real article. Colour schemes are also made use of to decorate food, particularly the sweets. A good chef will not be satisfied to produce dishes which tickle only the palate; they should also gladden the eyes, and their names should please the ears as well. The best example is a Cantonese dish called *Pi Yu Shan Hu* 碧玉珊瑚 which means "green jade and red coral". The green jade is represented by vegetable stems, and the red coral by fat of crabs. This dish is beautiful in appearance, delicious in taste, and in addition, elegant in name.

DINNER PARTIES

RESTAURANT DINNERS 酒 席

A dinner at a restaurant can be ordered in the form of a table d'hote 整 桌 or a la carte 小酌. The latter is only for dinners of a very informal nature among intimate friends, and must never be given in entertaining an honoured guest or in celebrating some important event.

A full course dinner usually consists of eight large and eight small dishes 八 大 八 小 with the addition of pastries, rice or noodles, and fruit. It is a long menu, and is, in truth, a great deal more than necessary. Ten years ago, however, such a menu would have been considered surprisingly short, as, at that time, a full table often consisted of about forty dishes or courses.

The dinner begins with four cold dishes which are placed on the table before the guests take their seats. Cold ham, an important item, is always placed before the guest of honour. Occasionally sliced duck takes the place of ham.

In recent years there has been a tendency to combine these four small dishes into one large dish called *Ping P'en* 拼盆. Following these, four hot fried dishes or *Ch'ao Ts'ai* 炒菜 will be served one at a time. These always consist of something in season.

Then comes the main part of the dinner, the eight large dishes. According to Chinese custom the best should be served first. Sharks' fins, being considered the foremost delicacy, therefore take the lead. In North China bird's nest ranks equally as high. A couple of other dishes are next served. Then comes the second important dish which is usually a roast, such as barbecued duck or suckling pig. The rest follow in turn, a fish and a soup always making the last items. Chicken soup is a favourite in the South, while the Northerners prefer duck soup. The meal concludes with rice served in small bowls, dainty pastries and a large bowl of some sweet liquid like hot orangeade or almond tea.

HOME DINNERS 家厨酒席

A higher standard of cooking is required in the preparation of a home dinner. Every detail

of the culinary art can be more conveniently
carried out in one's own kitchen. As it is more
important to aim at quality rather than quantity
it is usual to provide a dinner of only eight or
ten dishes, which should include a choice soup.
Some foreigners, perhaps mistakenly or joking-
ly, call a home dinner "coolie chow", but, as a
matter of fact, the most pleasing and tasty dishes
are often met with at these meals.

Since the inauguration of the New Life Move-
ment it has become a recognised practice to
entertain at home, the food being prepared on
the premises. If the host does not possess a
cook sufficiently skillful for this purpose, he
usually gets around the difficulty by enlisting
the services of some capable cook known to him.

It often happens that the cook thus secured
is in the employ of one of the host's many
friends: he borrows the cook, and at the same
time invites the employer to the dinner. At the
end of the repast the host will remark on the
excellence of the food served, while the friend,
whose cook's services have been requisitioned,
will say just the reverse. The other guests,
if ignorant of the arrangement, are naturally
astonished at the lack of modesty on the part

A Home Dinner

of their host, and the seeming rudeness on that of the friend. When the secret is disclosed, it is only right that the host should praise the accomplishments of his friend's cook, while the friend should remain modest in regard to them.

A dinner at home has many advantages over one at a restaurant. The guests can be made more comfortable, and are permitted greater leisure in the enjoyment of the repast. Cleanliness is more likely to be observed in the preparation of the food, thus making it more wholesome. Lastly, it is generally more economical.

When a regular dinner is given at home, the host, from modesty, always calls it "plain dinner" *Pien Fan* 便飯.

Plain Daily Meal

The daily meal is called *Chia Ch'ang Pien Fan* 家常便飯, i.e., ordinary plain home meal. For a family of five or six persons a daily meal usually consists of three meat dishes and two vegetables. Soup may or may not be served. The main point of difference is that during the daily meal, all the dishes and the rice are served at the same time. Chinese are taught from childhood to regard rice as the main item of a meal and to partake only sparingly of meat and vegetables.   Though there may be plenty of meat, children are always taught not to take too much of it.

TABLE MANNERS

The Analects state, "He who exercises government by means of his virtue may be compared to the North Polar Star, which retains its position, and all other stars always turn towards it." The Emperor was known as the Son of Heaven, and his throne was always placed on the North side of the Hall facing South. The highest seat is therefore situated in the North facing South. Consequently, in arranging seats we have to take the following into consideration:—

(a) A *K'ang* 炕 may be considered as a layman's throne. A "Long table" is a narrow high table on which offerings to God or to ancestors are placed. When there is either one of these two things in the room, the side on which it is placed is taken for granted as the North, regardless of its true direction.

(b) When both are absent from the room, the entrance is always regarded as the South.

North   North

2 Persons

3 Persons

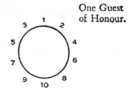

One Guest
of Honour.

4 Persons

5 Persons

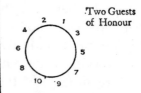

Two Guests
of Honour

6 Persons

7 Persons

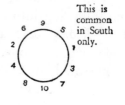

This is
common
in South
only.

8 Persons

Old Square Table
Arrangements

Round Table
Arrangements

At a round dinner table the seat of the guest of honour is on the North and that of the host opposite to him on the South. The left side is considered higher than the right. The reason is not known, but it is presumably due to the fact that the sun rises in the East which is on the left-hand side looking from North to South. To the left side of the guest of honour then, is the next seat in rank and to his right the third, and so on. Those who sit near the host are either minor guests or his very intimate friends.

In the South the seating arrangement amongst the merchants is different, the seat directly opposite the host being considered the next above the host himself. The guest of honour is seated on the left of the host two seats away, and the next in rank goes to the corresponding seat on the right.

Before the guests take their seats chopsticks, spoons, wine cups, saucers, and bone plates are arranged systematically in front of each seat. A set of these articles is supplied to each person, exclusively for his own use throughout the meal.

With the exception of four cold dishes which are placed on the table before the arrival of the guests, all the dishes are served one at a time,

each new dish being placed in the centre of the
table.   As soon as the second dish is brought
in, the first should be taken away.   Present-day
requirements call for the provision of a few
extra spoons, which are placed in convenient
positions on the table for the purpose of pick-
ing up food from the dishes in preference to
one's own chopsticks.   Two varieties of large
spoons are used, the porcelain ones for soup and
the silver ones for other food.   This new arrangement meets with general approval, as,
before its introduction, food used to be picked
up from the main dish with the aid of chopsticks
and transferred directly to the mouth.

When all the guests have arrived, the order
to "warm" the wine is given.   The wine commonly used in China is Shaohsing or rice wine,
and it must first be warmed.   When the wine
is brought in, the host announces the name of
the guest of honour, and fills his cup with wine,
indicating his seat at the same time.   This is
repeated with the second and the third guests,
and so on, until all the cups are filled except
that of the host himself.   To be polite the guest
of honour should return the compliment by
filling the host's cup.

When everyone is seated, the host takes his seat also. He then raises his wine cup saying *Ch'ing* 請 meaning "please". All the guests will then drink. After the drink the host again utters *Ch'ing* with a pair of chopsticks in his hand. The guest of honour then takes up his pair of chopsticks and begins to eat. His action will be followed by the other guests. Generally the host will wait until all his friends have had their share, as it is considered bad manners on his part to begin too soon. To enliven the proceedings the above ceremony may be repeated each time a new dish is served.

When the first main dish is brought in, usually sharks' fins, the host will request the guests to drain their cups saying *Kan Pei* 乾杯, literally, "Dry cup", or simply *Ch'ing*. The guest of honour should now take the opportunity to thank the host for his hospitality.

If it happens to be a special occasion, such as a wedding banquet, and there are a large number of guests and many tables, the host will visit every table with a cup of wine in his hand and drink with the guests. The first main dish is served only in the presence of the host. This rite is called "presenting" 献. A big banquet has three presentings, but, as a rule, the ordinary wedding feast has only one. Guests take the opportunity to thank the host and drink with him immediately after the presenting ceremony. The return of compliment is called *Ch'ou* 酢. After this, due ceremony is considered to have been observed, and all are at liberty to enjoy the repast at leisure.

Should, however, as often happens, any of the guests show some hesitation in helping himself, the host will attempt to remedy the situation by saying *Sui Pien* 隨 便 which means "please do not stand on ceremony". Except on formal occasions a Chinese dinner is by no means a staid affair. The average Chinese is not devoid of a sense of humour, and can be counted upon not to miss any opportunity of contributing towards the "fun" of the evening. One of the ways of putting life into the party is by means of the finger game. No compulsion is employed: the loser is penalized by having to drink either a cup for each individual match, or a cup for the best of three matches. These matches may be played between any two guests, but on certain occasions the host plays with each guest in turn, and each guest should do likewise.

To the foreigner, it may seem strange that the loser, and not the winner, should have the pleasure of drinking, but, if careful reflection be given to the matter, it will be agreed that the Chinese are wise in that their viewpoint, in this as in many other instances, is diametrically opposed to the Western.

It is said that as soon as the wine is in, restraint is out, so once the flow of wine has been thus started, it is naturally to be expected to lead to a certain amount of conviviality and hilarity during the rest of the evening's proceedings. We often wonder whether foreign cocktails are intended to serve the same purpose.

Following the main dishes, which always end with a large bowl of duck soup and a fish, rice and pastries are served, and, at the same time, the supply of wine is cut off. As a matter of fact, the rice is ldom touched, and the reason is obvious. The fruit item, which is usually very welcome, is partaken of in an adjoining room. At this point hot towels are handed round—a Chinese custom which serves a double purpose in that it replaces the modern finger bowl, and acts, at the same time, as a

signal to mark the end of a perfect evening.

The following rules governing table manners are translated from Chapter 1 of the old Chinese Classic — Book of Etiquette — written about 3,000 years ago.

DON'TS AT A CHINESE DINNER TABLE

1.	毋 摶 飯	Do not roll the rice into a ball.
2.	毋 放 飯	Do not bolt your food.
3.	毋 流 歠	Do not swill your soup.
4.	毋 咤 食	Do not eat audibly.
5.	毋 齧 骨	Do not crunch bones with your teeth.
6.	毋 反 魚 肉	Do not replace fish and meat which you have already tasted.
7.	毋 投 狗 骨	Do not throw bones to dogs.
8.	毋 固 獲	Do not make a grab at what you want.
9.	毋 揚 飯	Do not spread out the rice to cool.
10.	毋 嚃 羹	Do not draw particles of food in the soup through your mouth; use chopsticks for this purpose.
11.	毋 絮 羹	Do not stir or add condiments

Fig. 1

Fig. 2

Fig. 3

to the soup in the common bowl.

12.　毋　刺　齒　Do not pick your teeth.

How to Hold Chopsticks

Chopsticks are made use of to pick up morsels of food from a dish, and to aid in the transfer of rice from a bowl to the mouth. They are always in pairs, each stick being about 9 inches long, and they are so held in the hand that one is fixed in position while the other is movable. The correct way of holding them is as follows:—

Hold the fixed one in your hand as in Figure 1 opposite, making it firm by pressure between the inside of the thumb and the end of the fourth finger. Then hold the other, the movable one, as you would hold a pen, but in a more upright position, as in Figure 2.

Use the middle finger to perform the movements necessary, the tip of the thumb acting as a pivot. In this way the two sticks can be used to act as a pair of pincers for taking up the food.

Figure 3 shows the correct way of holding the two sticks.

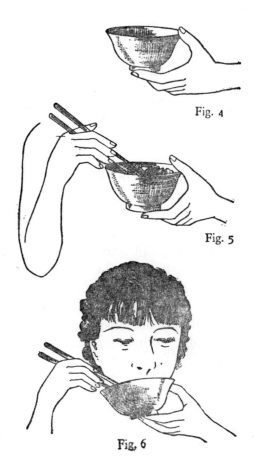

Fig. 4

Fig. 5

Fig. 6

How to Hold Rice Bowls

Hold the rice bowl with your left hand as shown in Figure 4. To get a firm grip the thumb should be placed on the upper rim and the first two fingers on the bottom of the bowl.

Figure 5 shows the position of the elbows while the right hand holds the chopsticks and the left hand holds the bowl.

Figure 6 indicates the correct position just at the point of eating. Certain definite rules are observed in regard to the manipulating of chopsticks and the rice bowl. Even the left-handed child is taught to hold his chopsticks with the right hand and the rice bowl in the left. On no account should the chopsticks be employed to shovel the rice from the bowl into the mouth; nor should the bowl be moved unduly. Only a gentle turn of the chopsticks by wrist action is needed to transfer the rice from the bowl to the mouth. The elbows should be kept as close as possible to the body, and should not be pointed outwards as they are likely to annoy your neighbours.

乾
杯 KAN PEi

TABLE SERVICE

A complete Chinese dinner service for ten persons consists of 148 pieces. This may be either of porcelain or silver, the latter being used only by wealthy families, while the porcelain is perhaps the more serviceable. Pewter articles were once used a great deal but they are now being rapidly displaced by the porcelain variety. Porcelain produced in Kiangsi Province is the best, because of the excellent quality of the clay available in the vicinity of *Poyang Lake* 鄱揚湖 where more than a dozen varieties can be found. The town Ching Te Chen 景德鎮, in Kiangsi, is responsible for nearly half of the porcelain in China. Its products are exported through the port of Kiukiang—hence they are called Kiukiang porcelains.

Ching Te Chen was one of the most important centres of the Chinese ceramic industry as far back as 200 A.D., and has since that date made the most beautiful china for the Imperial family. The famous "rice" pattern had its origin there.

The porcelain made in Kwangtung Province
廣東省 and exported through the city of Canton
廣州 is known as Canton porcelain. This is,
however, a grade inferior in quality to the
Kiangsi product. There are two distinct styles
of table crockery in use. The new style is thin,
shallow and round in shape. The decorations
consist generally of Chinese figures, flowers and
birds, or landscapes. White on both surfaces
is the common type, although the coloured
variety is always obtainable. The old style of
porcelain is thicker, deeper and usually hex-
agonal or octagonal in shape. The outer surface is usually dark blue or imperial yellow, and
covered with antique Chinese designs, while the
inner is generally of light blue colour.

Excellent copies of the old porcelain are now
made in Kiukiang. These are extremely effec-
tive as table decorations and are much admired
by foreigners.

Silver table sets are only seen in wealthy
families. Each set consists of two wine pots
and individual wine cups, soup spoons, pairs
of chopsticks, a small dish for nuts or water-
melon seeds, and another for soya bean sauce.
In addition to these a tiny tray is provided for

Kiangsi Porcelain

the wine cup and soup spoon, and a dainty rest
for the chopsticks. A table decorated with
beautifully coloured porcelain dishes and a
well-made set of the above silver articles pre-
sents a display at once highly attractive and
ornamental.

TEA

Tea might correctly be termed the national beverage of China as it is so generally drunk by all classes, and the habit is one of very long standing.

It is the Chinese custom even at the present day to welcome a guest with a cup of tea and this is observed by the high and low alike. Good tea is of a clear colour, greenish or reddish, and has a slightly astringent flavour. The poor quality is very light in colour and bitter in taste. There are an indefinite number of varieties of China tea, with a wide range of prices. According to the method of curing, tea is divided into two main classes, viz:—green and black tea.

Green tea leaves are dried and roasted as soon as they are picked, while the black variety is allowed to pass through a process of fermentation for a certain number of hours before softening and roasting. The best green tea leaves are picked before "grain rain" 穀雨 which falls about Easter time when they are still young. The leaves are tender and the aroma strong. The Province of Fukien produces the best green tea in China from a mountain called Wu-I. It is therefore called *Wu-I Ch'a* 武彝茶 . Lung *Ching Ch'a* 龍井茶 is another well-known green tea. It comes from the lake city of Hangchow in Chekiang, where chrysanthemum tea 杭菊 is also famous. Scented tea, such as Jasmine tea 茉莉茶 or *Hsiang P'ien* 香片 are much appreciated by foreigners.

Black tea is produced in many districts. The better known varieties are *Kee-mun* 祁門 from Kiangsi, *Liu-an* 六安 and *Wu-loong* 烏龍 from Anhui, and *Po-erh* 普洱 from Yunnan. Yet another popular kind of black tea is *Pekoe* 白毫 which is a small leaf with a fuzzy surface and is marketed either scented or unscented.

The golden rule of making tea is to boil the water, not the tea. Put the leaves in a Chinese tea cup, pour boiling water over them, and cover the cup with the lid. In a few minutes your cup of delicious tea is ready. Sugar and milk are never used in the Chinese style.

WINE AND SONG

No dinner is complete without wine, which brings joy and drives away depression, and makes the old feel young and the young still more youthful. Taken in moderation, it is undoubtedly an excellent stimulant. In the far north where the climate is cold and kaoliang abundant, Kaoliang wine, which is somewhat stronger than Russian vodka or English gin, is commonly drunk.

In Central China a milder drink known as Shaohsing wine—named after its producing centre in Chekiang—is very popular. It is the wine of China. It has another name *Hua Tiao* 花彫 meaning flower decoration, because the jars in which the wine is kept usually bear a floral decoration. When a girl is born, it is the common practice for the parents to make several jars of Shaohsing wine, the quantity depending upon the size of their purse, and keep them in a cool and dark room, until their daughter is married, so that on her wedding day, they will have at least some good old wine with which to entertain their guests.

In the South, where the climate is much warmer, a still milder drink known as *Liao Pan* 料半 meaning half strength, is commonly used. Stronger varieties, the double distilled 雙蒸 and triple distilled 三蒸 are, however, obtainable. The flavouring of the wine is usually added afterwards, such as orange blossom 橙花 and green plum 青梅.

Though Confucius was very particular in regard to food, his list of undesirable foodstuffs being a long one, he was not so with wine, as apparently all wines were acceptable to him. There are no records as to his capacity, but he is believed to have been a good drinker like the rest of those ancient scholars.

My own capacity does not exceed one wine cup of Shaohsing, so I am really not qualified to say much on the art of drinking. Perhaps it is well, for it is a subject in which I suspect our Western friends can give Eastern folk quite a few lessons.

In days gone by, good wine was named after an official in Chingchow. By a strange co-incidence, the best Shaohsing wine obtainable

at the wine merchant Wong Yu Ho in Shanghai
is called LL.D. wine, after a famous Chinese
lawyer who was one of his best customers. To
secure some of this brand for my own use I
have to go to the shop armed with a note from
my legal friend as I know full well that I would
not get it otherwise: the shop will not supply it
to anyone who they think will not appreciate it.

The lawyer is now in Geneva, but I do not
doubt that this shop continues to supply him
with his favourite wine.

According to our ideas tea should be drunk
in quiet surroundings, while wine should be
accompanied by song. This may be the reason
why restaurants are always noisy.

The renowned poets of old were, as a rule,
good drinkers. Among them I may mention
Li Po 李白, *T'ao Tsin* 陶潛, and *Pa Chu I*
白居易. Wine gave them inspiration, and,
when they drank enough, they wrote beautiful
verses, a great number of which are still recited
by school boys and girls of today.

Below is a song composed by a well-known
tippler of the past who used to cheat his wife to
get liquor. One day he told his wife that he
had made up his mind to give up drinking, but

Wine Pot and Cups

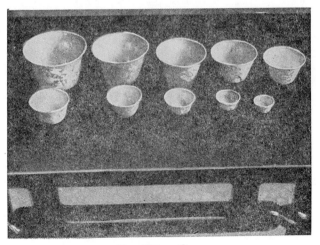

Ten Wine Cups

as he had had the habit for so long, it was only
fair to allow him one final session before quitting.
His wife was overjoyed to hear this, and proceed-
ed to search the whole town for the necessary
wine. When he got the wine, he immediately
drank the entire lot in one gulp, and then sang
the following verse referring to Chinese wine
measures:—

Liu Ling, Liu Ling (that's my name)	劉 伶 劉 伶
From drinking comes my fame;	以 酒 爲 名
A "hu" each bout I take,	一 飲 一 斛
Five "tou" I need to wake,	五 斗 鮮 醒
My wife she tries to plead,	婦 人 之 言
Her words are naught to heed.	切 不 可 聽

KITCHEN UTENSILS

1.	Rolling-Board	Kan Mien Pan
2.	Large Rolling-Pin	Ta Kan Mien Kun
3.	Small Rolling-Pin	Hsiao Kan Mien Kun
4.	Chopper	Ts'ai Tao
5.	Chopping-Block	Ts'ai Tun Tsu
6.	Meat Slice	Ch'an Tsu
7.	Bamboo Chopsticks	Chu K'uai Tsu
8.	Saucepan	Ta Kuo
9.	Steam Cooker	Cheng Lung
10.	Small Strainer	Hsiao Lou Shao
11.	Ladle	Shou Shao
12.	Large Strainer	Ta Lou Shao
13.	Chinese Frying-Pan	Ch'ao Shao
14.	Deep Earthenware Saucepan	Sha Kuo

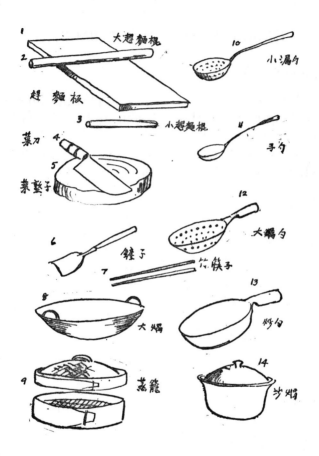

大趕麵棍
趕麵板
小趕麵棍
菜刀
菜墩子
鏟子
竹筷子
大鍋
蒸籠
小漏勺
手勺
大漏勺
炒勺
沙鍋

INGREDIENTS AND CONDIMENTS

Soya Sauce:

Soya sauce plays an important part in Chinese cooking as it imparts a flavour and taste totally different from salt.

In order to get the best flavour and taste it is always advisable to use the best quality.

Shao Hsing Wine:

When using wine in cooking it is best to use *Shaohsing* Wine. If not obtainable, sherry can take its place. It is never advisable to use wine which has turned sour. To preserve its flavour, keep in a cool place.

Winter Mushrooms:

How to soak dried mushrooms (*Tung Ku* 多菰):

Wash the necessary amount of mushrooms thoroughly two or three times, and soak them in boiling water for 15 minutes. Then pick off the stems, and they are ready for use.

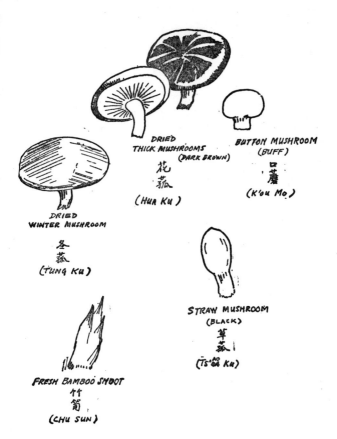

DRIED
THICK MUSHROOMS
(DARK BROWN)

花
菰

(HUA KU)

BUTTON MUSHROOM
(BUFF)

口
蘑

(K'OU MO)

DRIED
WINTER MUSHROOM

冬
菰

(TUNG KU)

STRAW MUSHROOM
(BLACK)

草
菰

(TS'AO KU)

FRESH BAMBOO SHOOT
竹
筍

(CHU SUN)

How to Boil Mushrooms:

Take ½lb. of soaked mushrooms, and cook them in a deep saucepan with 3 cups of cold water, 3 tsp. of soya sauce, 1 tsp. of salt, 2 tsp. of sugar, and ½ lb. of pork, for 10 minutes over a fast fire, and allow to simmer for 50 minutes. The mushrooms and sauce are then ready for use in such recipes as they are required for.

Three kinds of Mushrooms:—

1. Straw mushrooms *Ts'ao Ku* (草菰) grow from dried straws of glutinous rice. They are black in colour, and are usually cut in two halves and dried.

2. Winter mushrooms grow from wood. The thin kind is called *Tung Ku* (冬菰) and the thick *Hua Ku* (花菰). They are dark brown in colour when dried. Fresh mushrooms of this kind are very seldom seen in the market.

3. Button mushrooms can be obtained fresh or dried. They are called *K'ou Mo* (口蘑), and are excellent for soup making.

Red Haws (*Shan Cha Ping* 山渣餅):

Used for Sweet and Sour Pork, etc., according to the recipes, are crab-apples, with the cores taken out, crushed into thin round cakes after addition of sugar, and dried. These can be procured and, being in the dry form, easily stored.

Bamboo Shoots:

Tinned bamboo shoots can be used for cooking as they are, but fresh ones must be first boiled in water for about 10 to 15 minutes before use. The water should be discarded.

For those resident in America or in England who are desirous of securing ingredients for Chinese cooking, the numerous Chinese restaurants now existing in those countries should be able to supply them on request. If not obtainable, the following substitutes may be used:

Sweet and sour pickles may be substituted by foreign pickles.

Sesamum oil my be substituted by "Wesson oil".

Red haws may be substituted by crab-apple jelly.

Star-aniseed and red pepper may be substituted by bay leaves.

The measurements, such as cups, teaspoons,
etc., mentioned in the following recipes, are
exactly the same as those used in foreign
countries.

Ginger:

For the following recipes, when ginger is
used in tiny slices, it is measured by the tip of
a finger; when used in big slices, by the tip of
the thumb.

Chinese Onion:

The word stalk used in the recipes refers to
about two inches only, and not the full length.
When minced or finely chopped, it means a
length of about ¼ inch.

Selected Recipes

中饌珍腌

HOW TO MAKE A CUP OF TEA

(Hsiang Pien 香片)

Proportion:

1   Coffee-spoonful of tea leaves
1   Measuring cup of boiling water

Method:

Put the leaves into a Chinese tea-cup.
Then pour on water that has just boiled, and
    cover with the lid.   Allow it to stand for
    3 minutes, without stirring.   It is then
    ready for serving.

HOW TO COOK RICE

(Shao Fan 燒飯)

Proportion:

   1   Chinese bowl of rice

   2   Chinese bowls of water

Method:

Wash the rice thoroughly 4 or 5 times in
cold water. Put the rice in a deep saucepan, add the water, bring to boiling point,
and let it boil for 7 minutes. Then simmer
over a small fire for 30 minutes.

The above will make 3 bowls of rice.

FRIED RICE

(Shih Ch'in Ch'ao Fan 什錦炒飯)

Ingredients:

8	Bowls of cold cooked rice
1	Finely chopped onion
¼ lb.	Finely chopped ham (cooked)
8	Finely chopped mushrooms (previously soaked)
¼ lb.	Chicken meat (cooked and cut into small pieces)
3	Whole eggs, beaten up and fried until they are quite firm, then broken up into small pieces.
¼ lb.	Tinned green peas
¼ lb.	Shrimps (cooked)
¼ lb.	Tinned bamboo shoots, cut in squares
¼ lb.	Chinese cooked sausage, cut in squares.
½ cup	Lard.

Method:

Put ¼ cup of lard into a hot frying-pan with 1 teaspoonful of salt. Add the rice and fry for 5 minutes. Then turn out into a bowl.

Add another ¼ cup of lard. Fry the onion
until a light brown, then add the remaining ingredients and fry for 3 minutes.

Now add the rice, and 5 teaspoonfuls of soya
sauce and mix thoroughly.

Serve hot in a large bowl. The above
quantity is sufficient for 8 persons.

FOWL DISHES

(Ch'in Lei 禽 類)

GOLD COIN CHICKEN

(Chin Ch'ien Chi 金 錢 鷄)

Ingredients:

¼ lb. Chicken fillet (Sliced)

½ teaspoonful Cornflour

½ teaspoonful Salt   } Mix together

3 teaspoonfuls Wine

¼ lb. Roast Pork (sliced)

¼ lb. Cooked Ham (sliced)

¼ lb. Cooked Mushrooms (Tung Ku) whole

1/3 cup Lard

Method:

Transfix on a skewer, about the length of a pencil, pieces of chicken, ham, mushroom, and roast pork, one piece of each at a time, in the order mentioned.

The above material is sufficient for 4 such skewers.

Rub them well over with the lard, then toast them over an open fire for 15 minutes, as you would toast bread, or roast them in a quick oven for 15 minutes. Remove skewers before serving.

WALNUT CHICKEN

(Hê Tao Chi Ting 核桃鷄丁)

Ingredients:

- 1 lb. Chicken fillet (cut into squares)
- 1 Cup Walnuts
- 1 Slice Ham
- ½ Cup Lard
- a pinch of salt
- 2 teaspoonfuls wine ⎫
- ½ teaspoonful salt ⎬ Mix in chicken
- ½ teaspoonful corn flour ⎭

Method:

Blanch the walnuts in boiling water for 15 minutes, adding a pinch of salt. Take them out and fry them in deep fat until light brown. Allow to cool.

Now fry the chicken in ½ cup of lard for a minute. Remove and drain.

Using the lard left in the pan fry the chicken again with the walnuts and ham for a minute, then serve.

CHILI OIL CHICKEN AND SPINACH

(La Yu Chi Ting 辣油鷄丁)

Ingredients:

¾	lb. chicken fillet (cut into squares)
½	teaspoonful salt
½	teaspoonful corn flour
1½	tablespoonfuls water

Mix the above ingredients together

4	hot chilis (cut in halves)
1	lb. spinach
1	teaspoonful wine
1	teaspoonful soya sauce
½	teaspoonful salt
¾	cup lard

Method:

Heat ½ cup of lard in a frying pan, fry the hot chilis until brown, and remove them.

Using the same fat, fry the chicken. Add the wine and soya sauce.

Fry the spinach with ¼ cup of lard and salt for 2 minutes. Serve in a dish, the chicken on one half of the dish, and the spinach on the other, after garnishing with a little of the fried chilis chopped up.

STEWED CHESTNUT CHICKEN

(Li Tzu Mên Chi 栗子爛鷄)

Ingredients:

1	spring chicken (chopped with bone)
1	slice ginger
1	small stalk Chinese onion
1	cup chestnuts (cut in halves and boiled 15 minutes)
1	teaspoonfuls salt
6	teaspoonfuls soya sauce
1	teaspoonful sugar
1	teaspoonful wine
¼	cup lard.
2	cups water

Method:

Heat the lard in a frying-pan and fry the ginger, onion, then add the chicken, soya sauce, salt, sugar, wine, water.

Then simmer for ¾ of an hour.

Now add the boiled chestnuts and simmer for another 15 minutes.

Serve with gravy.

FRIED CHICKEN WITH PEPPER AND BROWN SAUCE

(Chiang Pao Chi Ting 醬泡鷄丁)

Ingredients:

¾	lb. chicken fillet	(cut in squares)
2	soaked mushrooms	(,, ,, ,,)
2	green peppers	(,, ,, ,,)
2	red chilis	(,, ,, ,,)
¾	cup lard.	
1	bamboo-shoot	(,, ,, ,,)
½	teaspoonful salt	
2	teaspoonfuls wine	
3	teaspoonfuls chiang 甜麵醬 (a thick brown sauce)	

Method:

Mix the chicken with salt, cornflour, wine, well.

Heat ½ cup of lard in hot frying-pan, fry the chicken for 2 minutes. Take out and drain.

Add ¼ cup lard and fry the chiang a little.
Fry the mushrooms, pepper, chilis, bam-
booshoot together for 2 minutes. Then
replace the chicken, fry another 1 minute.

Serve very hot.

VELVET CHICKEN (IMITATION)
(Fu Yung Chia Chi P'ien 芙蓉假鷄片)

Ingredients:

- 10 egg whites
- 1 lb. spinach
- a little shredded bamboo-shoot
- 1 teaspoonful salt
- 1 slice ham (finely chopped)
- 1¼ cup lard

Method:

Stir the egg whites up a little with the salt.

Heat the lard moderately in a pan, pour in the eggs and let it set. Remove and drain.

Leaving a cup of lard in the pan, fry the vegetables, and when they are cooked, drain away the liquid, and turn out on to a dish.

For the sauce you require:

> ½ teaspoonful salt ½ cup stock
> 2 teaspoonfuls corn flour

Method:

Put the stock in a hot pan, add the salt, and the corn flour mixed with a little water.

To this sauce add the cooked egg and stir for a second, pour this on top of the vegetables. Garnish with the ham and serve.

ROAST STUFFED CHICKEN

(K'ao Jang Chi 烤釀鷄)

Ingredients:

1	Spring chicken (boned)
1	lb. pork (minced)
1	Slice ginger (finely chopped)
1	Stalk Chinese onion (finely chopped)
1	Heaped teaspoonful corn flour
½	Cup water
1	Teaspoonful wine
1	Teaspoonful salt
½	Teaspoonful sugar
3	Teaspoonfuls soya sauce
¼	Cup lard

Method:

Mix well together the pork, ginger, onion corn flour, wine, salt, sugar, 2 teaspoonfuls soya sauce and ½ cup of water. Put this stuffing into the boned chicken. Roast in a hot oven with the lard and 1 teaspoonful soya sauce for ¾ hour. Cut in big slices before serving.

ROAST CHICKEN (BONELESS)

(Kuo Shao Chi 鍋燒鷄)

Ingredients:

1　Spring chicken
3　teaspoonfuls wine
5　teaspoonfuls soya sauce
3　teaspoonfuls cornflour

Method:

Boil the chicken for 1½ hours, then bone it, and let it stand until cold.

Make a paste with the cornflour, wine, and soya sauce. Rub this over the chicken, and fry it in deep fat until brown and crisp. Serve immediately.

VELVET CHICKEN WITH CORN
(Chi Jung Yü Mi 鷄蓉玉米)

Ingredients:

2   chicken breasts
1   small piece fat pork
1   tin sweet corn
1   slice cooked ham (finely chopped)
1   teaspoonful salt
1   teaspoonful wine
3¾ cups chicken stock
1   teaspoonful lard
3   teaspoonfuls cornflour

Method:

Mince the chicken and pork well together.

Add ½ teaspoonful salt, wine, cornflour and ¾ cup stock.

Put the rest of the stock and salt in a pan, and boil. When boiling, add the sweet corn and the chicken and pork mixture, and bring to the boil again, stirring constantly for about 3 minutes.

Lastly, add the lard, and stir thoroughly.

Garnish with the ham, and serve in a deep bowl.

STUFFED MUSHROOMS

(Jang Tung Ku 釀冬菰)

Ingredients:

- 16 Mushrooms (soaked and cooked)
- 2 Chicken breats (minced)
- ¼ lb. pork fat (minced)
- 1 White of egg
- 1 Slice cooked ham (finely chopped)
- 1 Teaspoonful salt
- ¾ Cup meat stock
- 3 Teaspoonfuls soya sauce
- 1 Teaspoonful sugar
- 3 Teaspoonfuls wine
- 2 Teaspoonfuls corn flour
- 1 Teaspoonful lard

Method:

Add to the chicken 2 teaspoonfuls wine, ½ teaspoonful salt, 1 teaspoonful cornflour, the egg white, ham and ¼ cup meat stock, and mix thoroughly.

Cook the mushrooms in sufficient water.
Add the soya sauce, sugar, and ½ teaspoonful salt, and simmer for 1 hour.
Take out the mushrooms and allow to
cool.

Now stuff each mushroom with the chicken
filling, place in a double boiler and steam
for 10 minutes. Serve with the sauce as
made below.

Put the rest of the meat stock in a frying pan,
add ½ tsp. salt. Mix the cornflour with
a little water in a cup. Add this slowly,
together with the lard.

PINEAPPLE AND GINGER DUCK
(Po Lo Chiang Ya Tzu 波蘿薑鴨子)

Ingredients:

1   Spring Duck (about 3 lbs.)
1   Small tin Pineapple
6   Pieces Ginger (tinned)
1   Teaspoonful salt

Method:

Steam the whole duck for 2½ hours, then remove it and allow to cool.

Now cut it up into large slices, and arrange these in the centre of a big dish.

Also cut the pineapple and ginger into thick slices and arrange them alternately round the duck.

Sauce Ingredients:

1½ Teaspoonfuls Cornflour
1   Cup of Pineapple juice (from the tin)
½   Cup of Ginger juice (from the tin)

Method:

Heat the pineapple and ginger juice in a frying-pan for a little while, then add the cornflour mixed with a little cold water to thicken it. Pour this on top of the duck before serving.

ROAST CRISP DUCK

(Ts'ui P'i Ya Tzu 脆皮鴨子)

Ingredients:

  1   duck (about 3 lbs.)
  5   teaspoonfuls soya sauce
 10   teaspoonfuls salt
  1   stalk Chinese onion
  1   small clove garlic
  1   big slice ginger
  3   small pieces aniseed (pa chiao 八角)

Method:

Cover the duck with cold water in a deep
saucepan. Add the ingredients, and bring
to the boil. Then simmer for 1½ hours.
Remove the duck. When cold fry it in deep
fat about 6 minutes, keeping it well basted,
till a golden brown.
Serve while very hot and crisp, either serve
whole, or cut it up before serving.

RED SAUCE DUCK

(Hung Shao P'a Ya 紅燒扒鴨)

Ingredients:

1	duck (3 lbs.)
1	large slice ginger
1	stalk Chinese onion
5	large mushrooms (soaked)
2	teaspoonfuls sesamum oil
3	teaspoonfuls salt
3	teaspoonfuls wine
3	teaspoonfuls soya sauce
2	teaspoonfuls sugar

Method:

Place the duck in a deep saucepan, add the rest of the ingredients and sufficient water to cover the duck.

Bring to the boil, then allow to simmer for 1½ hours. Serve whole, with gravy.

FRIED DUCK LIVER

(Ch'ao Ya Kan 炒鴨肝)

Ingredients:

        8   duck livers (sliced)
        2   soaked mushrooms (sliced)
        1   bamboo-shoot (shredded)
        1   small stalk Chinese onion (sliced)
        1   small slice ginger
      ½   clove garlic
        a   dash of pepper
      1/3 cup lard
      ½   teaspoonful salt
      ½   teaspoonful sugar
      1½ teaspoonfuls cornflour
        1   teaspoonful sesamum oil
        1   teaspoonful wine
        3   teaspoonfuls soya sauce
      1/3 cup stock

Method:

To the liver add a dash of pepper, salt and
    1 teaspoonful of cornflour, and mix well.
Heat the lard in a frying-pan, fry the liver
    for a minute, remove and drain.

Using the same lard left in the pan, fry the garlic, ginger, and onion, and brown a little.

Add the bamboo-shoot, mushrooms, soya sauce, sugar, sesamum oil, and stock, and allow to cook for 2 minutes.

Now replace the liver in the pan with the rest. Finally add the wine, and ½ teaspoonful of cornflour mixed with a little cold water.

FRIED WILD DUCK

(Ch'ao Shui Ya P'ien 炒水鴨片)

Ingredients:

2	ducks (breasts only sliced)
2	large soaked mushrooms (sliced)
1	bamboo shoot (sliced)
1	teaspoonful sesamum oil
1	teaspoonful sugar
a	dash of pepper
½	teaspoonful cornflour.
1	teaspoonful salt
1	teaspoonful wine
5	dessert spoonfuls cold water.
1/3 cup lard	

Method:

To the duck meat add ½ teaspoonful of salt
and a dash of pepper, then mix thoroughly
with cornflour and water.

Put ⅛ cup lard into a hot pan, and fry the
mushrooms and bamboo shoot, with ½
teaspoonful of salt and sugar. Turn out
into a dish,

Add the rest of the lard to the pan, fry the duck meat quickly for a minute. Drain off fat and add the wine and sesamum oil, together with mushrooms and bamboo shoot.

MINCED PIGEON

(Kê Tzu Sung 鴿子松)

Ingredients:

6	Pigeons (coarsely minced) only meat
4	small mushrooms (soaked and chopped)
10	water chestnuts
1	bamboo-shoot (finely diced)
1	stalk celery (finely chopped)
¼	lb. vermicelli (fried in deep fat)
1	stalk chopped Chinese onion
1	teaspoonful wine
1	teaspoonful salt
2½	teaspoonfuls cornflour
½	cup meat stock
3	teaspoonfuls soya sauce
½	teaspoonful sugar
1/3	cup lard

Method:

Mix ½ teaspoonful salt and ½ teaspoonful
  cornflour with the minced pigeon.
Heat the lard in a frying-pan, and brown
  the onion. Then fry the minced pigeon,

and add the soya sauce, sugar, celery, bamboo-shoot, water chestnuts, mush-rooms, meat stock, wine, and the rest of the salt.

Mix 2 teaspoonfuls of cornflour with a little water, and add to the contents of the pan.

Now break up the fried vermicelli with the fingers, place on a dish, and pour the pigeon mixture over it for serving.

MEAT DISHES

FRIED BEEF FILLET

(Ch'ao Niu Li Chi 炒牛里肌)

Ingredients:

1½ lb. beef fillet (sliced)
1   white of egg
1   small cauliflower (cooked sliced)
1   large onion (sliced)
½   cup lard
2   teaspoonfuls salt
a   dash of pepper
2   teaspoonfuls wine
2   teaspoonfuls soya sauce
2   teaspoonfuls cornflour
20   teaspoonfuls cold water
1   green pepper (sliced)

Method:

Mix the beef well with the pepper, cornflour,
salt and 1 teaspoonful of wine. Add the
egg white, and water to make the pieces
adhere. Heat the lard in a frying-pan,
and when boiling hot fry the beef for a
minute. Remove and drain, leaving a
little lard in the pan. Fry the onion to a

light brown, and then add cauliflower, green pepper and soya sauce. Now replace the beef in the pan, and 1 teaspoonful wine, stir well with the ingredients for about two minutes, and serve.

EGG AND BEEF OMELETS

(Chien Chi Tan Chiao 煎鷄蛋角)

Ingredients:

8 whole eggs lightly beaten
1 lb. lean minced beef ⎫
½ teaspoonful cornflour ⎬ Mix well together
½ teaspoonful salt ⎪
1 teaspoonful wine ⎭
2 teaspoonfuls soya sauce
½ teaspoonful sugar
½ onion cut up (very finely)
1/3 cup lard

Method:

Brown the onion in ¼ cup of lard, then put in the meat mixture and fry. Add the soya sauce, and sugar. When the meat is nicely browned, turn it out on to a dish.

Add a little more lard. When very hot, pour in about 1 teaspoonful of beaten egg.

Allow it to set slightly, then place a small quantity of the meat mixture on it, fold over, and fry. Repeat this until all the egg is used up. This is enough for about 20 individual omelets.

STUFFED GREEN PEPPER

(Niu Jou Jang La Chiao 牛肉釀辣椒)

Ingredients:

1 lb. green peppers (seeds removed)
1½ lb. minced beef
1 piece Chinese onion, (chopped finely)
1 small slice ginger, chopped finely
2 teaspoonfuls wine
2 teaspoonfuls salt
4 teaspoonfuls soya sauce
1 teaspoonful cornflour
¼ cup lard
1 cup of stock
1 teaspoonful (heaped) sugar
2 teaspoonfuls sesamum oil
20 teaspoonfuls water

Method:

Mix the beef with onion, ginger, wine, salt,
cornflour, 2 teaspoonfuls of soya sauce,
sesamum oil and cold water well. Stuff
the peppers with the mixture. Saute in
¼ cup of lard in a hot frying-pan, add 2
teaspoonfuls of soya sauce, sugar, 1 cup
of stock, turn into a deep saucepan, bring
to a boil, and simmer for about 30 minutes.

BROWN SAUCE BEEF

(Kuo Shao Niu Jou 鍋燒牛肉)

Ingredients:

  1½ lb. beef (ribs)
  1   clove garlic
  1   piece ginger
  1   stalk Chinese onion
  1   grain aniseed (Pa Chiao 八角)
  2   teaspoonfuls sesamum oil
  2   teaspoonfuls salt
  1   teaspoonful sugar
  6   teaspoonfuls cornflour
  2   teaspoonfuls soya sauce
  1   egg

Method:

To the beef in a deep saucepan, add all the ingredients (except the cornflour) and enough water to cover it.

Bring to the boil and then simmer for 3 hours. Take the beef out. Make a paste with the cornflour, egg and the gravy from the beef, and cover the beef with it. Then fry the beef in deep fat until golden brown. Serve in slices.

STEWED SHIN OF BEEF

(Hung Shao Niu Jou 紅燒牛肉)

Ingredients:

2	lb. shin of beef
	dash of pepper
1	large slice ginger
1	clove garlic
1	stalk Chinese onion
10	teaspoonfuls soya sauce
1	teaspoonful sesamum oil
2	teaspoonfuls salt
2	teaspoonfuls sugar

Method:

Saute the above ingredients together for a few minutes. Turn into a deep saucepan, and add sufficient water to cover the meat. Bring to the boil. Simmer for 3 hours.

Slice and serve with the gravy.

SWEET AND SOUR PORK (boneless)

(T'ang Ts'u P'ai Ku 糖醋排骨)

Ingredients:

2   lb. loin of pork (boned)
1   teaspoonful Chinese wine
6   teaspoonfuls (heaped) cornflour
1   teaspoonful salt
3   teaspoonfuls soya sauce

The above are mixed together.

Method:

Cut the pork into fairly large squares and mix well with the above ingredients. Fry in deep fat until crisp, and a golden brown. Drain and turn out on a plate.

Sauce Ingredients:

6   pieces red haws (shan cha ping 山渣餅)
½   cup Chinese sweet and sour mixed pickles (or any other kind)
1   small piece Chinese onion (finely chopped)
⅛   cup lard
¼   cup vinegar

6	teaspoonfuls sugar
½	cup water
¼	clove garlic (finely chopped)
3	teaspoonfuls soya sauce
1½	teaspoonfuls cornflour

Method:

Heat the lard in a pan, brown the onion and
garlic a little.   Pour in the above ingredients, adding the cornflour previously
mixed with a little water, slowly, and
stirring, for 1 minute.

Then pour this sauce over the pork.   Serve
very hot, while the pork is crisp.   The
above quantity is sufficient for 6-8 persons.

RED SAUCE RUMP OF PORK

(P'a Chou Tzu 扒肘子)

Ingredients:

2	lb. Pork Rump
1	large piece ginger
½	stalk Chinese onion
¼	cup lard
3	teaspoonfuls soya sauce
2	teaspoonfuls salt
2	teaspoonfuls sugar
1	teaspoonful sesamum oil

Method:

Heat the lard in a frying-pan. Fry the rump with the ginger and onion. Then add the soya sauce, frying for about 5 minutes. Now turn out into a deep saucepan, add the salt and sugar, and sufficient water to cover. Bring to the boil, and allow to simmer for 2 hours. Serve with gravy.

STEWED MEAT-BALLS WITH
SHANTUNG CABBAGE

(Hung Shao Shih Tzu T'ou 紅燒獅子頭)

Meat Balls:

Ingredients:

1	lb. beef or pork (finely minced)
1	small slice ginger (chopped)
1	small stalk Chinese onion (chopped)
1	teaspoonful wine
2	teaspoonfuls cornflour
1	teaspoonful sesamum oil
3	teaspoonfuls water
½	teaspoonful salt
1/3	cup lard

Method:

Mix the above ingredients (except the lard)
    thoroughly into a stiff mass, then make
    into 4 large meat-balls.

Heat the lard in a pan, and saute the meat-
    balls until golden brown on both sides,
leave in a dish.

Cabbage:

Ingredients:

- 2   heads of cabbage (coarsely chopped)
- 6   teaspoonfuls soya sauce
- 1   cup stock
- 2   teaspoonfuls sugar
- ½   teaspoonful salt

Method:

Saute the cabbage in the fat left in the pan for 2 to 3 minutes, after adding the soya sauce, sugar, salt and stock. Turn out into a deep pan, place the meat-balls on top of the cabbage, and simmer for one hour.

STEWED RICE FLOUR PORK

(Mi Fên Jou 米粉肉)

Ingredients:

>   1   cup uncooked rice
>   1½ lb. streaky pork
>   1   piece ginger (finely chopped)
>   1   stalk Chinese onion (finely chopped)
>   ½   cup water
>   2   teaspoonfuls sesamum oil
>   4   teaspoonfuls soya sauce
>   ½   teaspoonful sugar
>   ½   teaspoonful salt.

Method:

Fry the rice in a hot dry pan, then pulveris
it. Put the powder into a bowl, add th
ginger, onion, salt, sugar, soya sauce
sesamum oil and water to make into
paste. Boil the pork for one hour, the
cut it up into thin slices. These are se
in a deep bowl side by side, with a laye
of the paste intervening, and with th
skin surface downwards. They are the

steamed for 2½ hours, with a thick slice
of ginger and a large piece of Chinese
onion. The whole is turned out on to a
dish, the lower side up, for serving.

ROAST SHASLICK PORK

(Ch'a Shao Jou叉燒肉)

Ingredients:

1½ lb. loin pork
a   dash of pepper
1   small stalk Chinese onion
1   slice ginger
¼   teaspoonful thick sauce (chiang)
½   teaspoonful sugar
5   teaspoonfuls soya sauce
1   teaspoonful wine
½   teaspoonful salt

Method:

Remove the bone from the pork. Cut it into
strips about 4 inches long. Mix all the
ingredients with the pork thoroughly and
allow to soak for ½ an hour.

Roast in a hot oven for 10 minutes, then turn
the meat over, and roast for another 5-10
minutes.

Slice before serving.

STEWED PORK WITH BAMBOO SHOOTS

(Hung Mên Wu Hua Chu Jou
紅 燜 五 花 猪 肉)

Ingredients:

½	lb. pork (Boiled 1 hour, then cut into squares)
2	Bamboo shoots (cut into squares)
1	small Chinese onion
2	soaked mushrooms (cut into squares)
½	clove garlic
1	slice ginger
2	teaspoonfuls sugar
2	cups water
10	teaspoonfuls soya sauce
1	teaspoonful salt
¼	cup lard

Method:

Heat the lard in a frying-pan, fry the ginger, garlic, and onion for a minute.

Add mushrooms, bamboo-shoots, and pork, then the salt, sugar, soya sauce and cold water, and cook for about 3 minutes.

Turn out into a deep saucepan, and simmer for 1½ hours.

Serve with gravy.

SEAFOOD DISHES

(Hai Hsien Lei 海鮮類)

BROWN SAUCE MANDARIN FISH
(Hung Shao Kuei Yü 紅燒桂魚)

Ingredients:

1	Mandarin Fish (about 2 lbs.)		
1	slice Ginger		
1	small stalk Chinese onion		
1	large clove Garlic		
6	Mshrooms (soaked)		
½	Bamboo shoot (sliced)		
1/3	cup Lard	7 tsps.	Soya sauce
1	teaspoonful Salt	2 tsps.	Wine
¼	lb. fat Pork (cut in squares)		
1	cup Meat stock		
½	teaspoonful Sugar 1 piece Star aniseed		

Method:

Heat the lard in a frying-pan, and saute the
fish, which has been previously scored, for
5 minutes until it is brown on both sides.

Add in the ginger, onion, garlic, mushrooms,
bamboo shoot, soya sauce, salt, wine, fat
pork, and meat stock. Cook for a while,
finally add the sugar and aniseed. Bring
to the boil, then simmer for half an hour
with a cover on the frying-pan. Serve the
fish whole.

FRIED FISH WITH SOUR SAUCE

(Cha Sung Shu Yü 炸松鼠魚)

Ingredients:

1   Mandarin fish (about 3 lbs.)
1   small stalk Chinese onion
1   small slice ginger
3   teaspoonfuls sugar
8   ,,   cornflour
1   teaspoonful salt
2   teaspoonfuls wine
2   ,,   soya sauce
¼   cup vinegar
¼   cup lard
¼   lb. pork (sliced)

Method:

Bone the fish and score the outside. Add the
    wine, and salt.
Rub thoroughly with 6 teaspoonfuls of corn-
    flour and fry the fish until golden brown
    and crisp. Now make the sauce as
    follows:—

Heat the lard in a frying pan. Fry the
ginger and onion a little, then add 2 teaspoonfuls soya sauce, the vinegar, sugar
and sliced pork.

Mix 2 teaspoonfuls of cornflour with a little
water, and add slowly, stirring all the
time, then pour the sauce on the fish and
serve.

SMOKED FISH

(Hsün Yü 燻魚)

Ingredients:

   1½ lb. yellow fish or any other fish (cut in
        large slices)
   1   large slice ginger
   1   large stalk Chinese onion
   1   clove garlic
   a   dash of pepper
   8   teaspoonfuls soya sauce
   1   teaspoonful sesamum oil
   3   teaspoonfuls Chinese wine
   2   teaspoonfuls sugar

Method:

   Soak the fish with the above ingredients for
      one hour. Fry the fish, piece by piece,
      in deep fat, until golden brown.

Sauce:

   The sauce for the fish is made by mixing
      together:
   2   teaspoonfuls soya sauce
   ½   teaspoonful salt
   1   teaspoonful sugar
   1/3 cup stock

Method:

Fry the fish again in ¼ cup of lard, then add the above sauce, and cook until the sauce has evaporated. The fish can be served either hot or cold.

FRIED MINCED FISH

(Ch'ao Yü Sung 炒魚松)

Ingredients:

½	lb. fish (minced)
1	Chinese onion (finely chopped)
1	thin slice ginger (finely chopped)
1	egg white
1	heaped teaspoonful cornflour
½	lb. turnips (cooked and shredded)
1/3	cup lard
1	teaspoonful salt
4	teaspoonfuls wine
1	teaspoonful soya sauce
½	teaspoonful sugar
½	cup peanuts (ground)
a	dash of pepper.

Method:

Mix the fish well with a dash of pepper, ½
teaspoonful of salt, the cornflour, 3 teaspoonfuls of wine and white of egg.

Heat ½ cup of the lard in a frying-pan, fry
the turnips for 3 or 4 minutes, adding
½ teaspoonful of salt. Then add 1 tea-

spoonful soya sauce, $\frac{1}{2}$ teaspoonful of
sugar, and fry for another few minutes.
Turn out into a dish.

Put the rest of the lard into the pan, brown
the ginger and onion a little, then fry the
fish mixture together until it becomes
lumpy.

Add 1 teaspoonful of wine and cook for a
minute. Pour this out on top of the
turnips, garnish with the ground peanuts
and serve.

WHITE SAUCE FISH (SOUR)
(Wu Liu Kuei Yü 五柳桂魚)

Ingredients:

- 1   whole mandarin fish (scored)
- 1   small Chinese onion
- 1   small piece ginger
- ½   clove garlic
- 2   teaspoonfuls sweet and sour pickles (Chinese or foreign)
- 1/3   cup vinegar (white)
- 2   teaspoonfuls cornflour
- ½   teaspoonful salt
- 6   teaspoonfuls sugar
- ½   cup fish stock
- ¼   cup lard

Method:

Put the fish in a pan of boiling water and boil for 15 minutes. Leavce it in a dish.

Sauce:

Heat half of the lard in a pan, fry the ginger, onion, and garlic together with the vinegar, stock, sugar, salt and pickles. Now mix the cornflour with a little cold water, and add it to the contents of the pan. Finally add the other half of the lard. Pour this sauce over the fish and serve.

FRIED FISH CAKES
(Chien Yü Ping 煎魚餅)

Ingredients:

¼	lb. fish (minced)
¼	cup dry shrimps (pounded)
1	tinned bamboo-shoot (coarsely sliced)
8	small soaked mushrooms
1	slice ham (cut in big pieces)
¼	cup lard
¼	cup stock
1	teaspoonful salt
½	teaspoonful sugar
1	teaspoonful wine
1	teaspoonful cornflour
2	teaspoonfuls soya sauce
1	teaspoonful sesamum oil

Method:

Mix the fish well with ½ teaspoonful salt, ½ teaspoonful cornflour, ¼ cup dry shrimps, and ¼ cup stock. Shape into small cakes. Heat the lard in a pan, and saute the cakes on both sides. Turn out into a dish.

Using the same fat, fry the bamboo-shoot,
  mushrooms, and ham for a minute. Add
  the sugar, soya sauce, wine, and the rest
  of the salt. Replace the fish cakes.
Mix ½ teaspoonful of cornflour with a little
  water, and add slowly. Lastly add the
  sesamum oil to flavour.

BRAISED SHRIMPS

(Hui Hsia Jen 燴 蝦 仁)

Ingredients:

- ½ lb. shrimps (shelled)
- 6 cooked water chestnuts (cut into small squares)
- 4 cooked mushrooms (cut into small squares)
- ½ cup peas (tinned)
- 2 slices cooked Chinese ham (cut into small squares)
- 1 tiny piece ginger (chopped finely)
- 1 tiny piece Chinese onion (chopped finely)
- 1 teaspoonful salt
- 2 teaspoonfuls cornflour
- 2 teaspoonfuls soya sauce
- 2 teaspoonfuls wine
- 1 teaspoonful sesamum oil
- 1/3 cup lard
- 1 cup stock

Method:

> Heat the lard in a frying-pan, and fry the
> shrimps a little together with the ginger,
> onion, soya sauce, wine, stock and salt.
>
> Add the water chestnuts, mushrooms, peas
> and ham. Now mix the cornflour with
> a little cold water and add it to the mix-
> ture.
>
> Finally add the sesamum oil. Fry altogether
> 3 minutes.

SHRIMP CAKES

(Chien Hsia Ping 煎 蝦 餅)

Ingredients:

1½ lb. pounded shrimps
1   slice ginger minced
1   small piece minced Chinese onion
10   pieces water chestnuts (remove skins and pound)
1   whole egg
a   dash of pepper
1½ teaspoonfuls salt
1   heaped teaspoonful cornflour
1/3 cup cold water or stock
1   Chinese cabbage, coarsely cut and part boiled

Method:

Mix all the above ingredients together with chopsticks. Shape into small flat cakes, and saute in hot lard until a nice golden colour on both sides.

Using the same lard fry the cabbage with a teaspoonful of salt for two minutes. Replace the shrimp cakes and fry altogether for another minute: then serve.

FRIED SHRIMP BALLS

(Cha Hsia Ch'iu 炸蝦球)

Ingredients:

> 1¼ lb. shrimps (shelled and minced)
> 6   water chestnuts (chopped finely)
> 1   slice ginger (chopped finely)
> 1   egg white
> a   little Chinese onion (chopped finely)
> 1   teaspoonful salt
> 1   teaspoonful cornflour
> 3   teaspoonfuls wine
> 1   teaspoonful sesamum oil
> a   dash of pepper

Method:

Mix the above ingredients well, shape into balls, and fry them in deep fat until golden brown.

STUFFED CLAMS

(Jang Hai Kê Li 釀海蛤蜊)

Ingredients:

2½ lb. clams (with shell)
¼   lb. fat pork or beef (minced)
1   slice ginger (finely chooped)
1   tiny piece Chinese onion (finely chopped)
3   teaspoonfuls wine
½   teaspoonful salt
½   teaspoonful sugar
1   teaspoonful soya sauce
¼   cup stock
⅛   cup lard

Method:

Pour boiling water over the clams and remove them from their shells. Mince the clams and the pork together.

Add to the mince the ginger, onion, wine, salt, sugar, and soya sauce, and mix well.

Stuff the mixture into the empty shells. Place these in a baking dish containing the lard and stock, and back in a hot oven for 10 minutes.

CRAB OMELET

(Fu Jung Hsieh Jou 芙蓉蟹肉)

Ingredients:

2	crabs (cooked and shelled)
4	eggs
1	small Chinese onion (chopped finely)
1	teaspoonful salt
1/3	cup lard

Method:

Heat the lard in a frying pan, and brown the
onion.

Beat the eggs lightly in a bowl, add the crab-
meat and salt, and fry together for 2
minutes. Serve hot.

CRAB FAT WITH GREEN VEGETABLES
(*Green Jade and Red Coral*)

(Pi Yü Shan Hu 碧玉珊瑚)

Ingredients:

½	lb. crab fat (cooked)
3½	lbs. Mustard Greens (only young stems) or any other green vegetables
1	slice ginger
1	teaspoonful sugar
1/3	cup lard
1	teaspoonful salt
3	teaspoonfuls wine
4	teaspoonfuls soya sauce

Method:

Heat the lard in the frying-pan. Fry the ginger a little, then remove the ginger. Add the vegetable, salt, wine, soya sauce and sugar, then add the crab fat. Fry for 3 mins. Serve while it is hot.

VEGETABLE DISHES

(Ts'ai Shu Lei 菜 蔬 類)

TIENTSIN CABBAGE WITH CHESTNUTS

(Hung Shao Li Tzu Pai Ts'ai 紅燒栗子白菜)

Ingredients:

2	stalks of Tientsin cabbage (only heart) (cut into coarse pieces)
10	medium sized mushrooms (soaked and cooked)
1	cup cooked chestnuts
1	teaspoonful salt
¼	cup stock
6	teaspoonfuls soya sauce
2	teaspoonfuls sugar
½	cup lard

Method:

Cut the chestnuts into halves with the shell, boil them for 10 minutes, and then remove the shells.

Place the lard in a frying pan, when very hot, put in the cabbage and mushrooms, fry slowly for about 10 minutes. Then add the salt, sugar, soya sauce and stock, and cook all together for 5 minutes.

Finally add the chestnuts, and cook for a further 5 minutes.

SOUR TIENTSIN CABBAGE

(Suan La Pai Ts'ai 酸辣白菜)

Ingredients:

1	lb. Tientsin cabbage (hearts only)
2	hot chilis (sliced)
1	teaspoonful Hua Chiao (花椒) (red pepper)
½	teaspoonful cornflour
1	teaspoonful salt
2	teaspoonfuls soya sauce
1	teaspoonful sesamum oil
1/3	cup vinegar (white)
½	cup lard

Method:

Heat the lard in a pan. Fry the Hua Chiao a little, then remove it.

Use the same fat, and fry the chilis and cabbage for 3 minutes. Then add the rest of the ingredients, and cook for another 2 minutes.

Serve warm.

FRIED MUSTARD GREENS

(Ch'ao Chieh Lan Ts'ai 炒芥蘭菜)

Ingredients:

    3½ lbs. Mustard Greens (only heart)
    1   big slice ginger
    1   teaspoonful sugar
    ¼   cup lard
    1   teaspoonful salt
    3   teaspoonfuls wine
    4   teaspoonfuls soya sauce

Method:

Heat the lard in a frying-pan. Fry the
ginger a little, then remove the ginger.
Add the vegetable, salt, wine, soya sauce
and sugar. Stir the mixture continuously
over a hot fire, and cook for 3 minutes.
The vegetable should be crisp and green.

BRAISED CHINESE VEGETABLES

(Mên Yu Ts'ai 燜油菜)

Ingredients:

Hearts of 2 lbs. Chinese cabbage (Yu Ts'ai)
    coarsely sliced
  2   tinned bamboo-shoots (sliced thinly)
  8   large mushrooms (soaked and cooked
      and cut up into halves)
  1   slice ginger
1½ teaspoonfuls salt
½   cup lard
  1   cup stock

Method:

Fry the ginger in hot lard, discard the ginger.
  Then add the salt and vegetables.
Fry just a little, mixing well together, lastly
  add stock. Put all into a deep saucepan,
  and simmer for about 15 minutes.

BRAISED FRESH MUSHROOMS WITH CHINESE CABBAGE

(Hui K'ou Mo Yu Ts'ai 燴口磨油菜)

Ingredients:

1	heart of cabbage (boiled)
1	bamboo-shoot (sliced)
½	lb. fresh mushrooms (cooked)
2	teaspoonfuls cornflour
½	teaspoonful salt
¼	cup lard

Method:

Boil the mushrooms in about 2 cups of cold water for 5 minutes. Heat the lard in a frying-pan, add salt and the mushrooms together with the water they were cooked in. Then add the cabbage and bamboo-shoot, and allow to cook for 10 minutes. Mix the cornflour with a little water and add it slowly to the mixture.

FOREIGN CABBAGE

(Hung Shao Yang Pai Ts'ai 紅燒洋白菜)

Ingredients:

2   cabbage hearts (broken up)
6   teaspoonfuls soya sauce
2   teaspoonfuls sugar
1   teaspoonful salt
½   cup lard

Method:

Heat the lard in a frying pan. Put in the
   cabbage and cook for 5 minutes. Then
   add the soya sauce, sugar and salt, and
   cook for a further 10 minutes, until the
   cabbage contains practically no water.

BRAISED BAMBOO-SHOOTS

(Yu Mên Sun 油燜筍)

Ingredients:

10	bamboo-shoots (cut up and boiled for 15 minutes)
½	teaspoonful salt
1	heaped teaspoonful sugar
5	teaspoonfuls soya sauce
1	teaspoonful wine
¼	cup lard
¼	cup stock

Method:

Heat the lard in a frying-pan and fry the bamboo-shoots (previously boiled) with the salt, sugar, soya sauce, wine and stock.

Turn out into a deep saucepan, bring to the boil, then simmer for 20 minutes.

Serve hot.

WHITE SAUCE WATER BAMBOO-SHOOTS

(Pai Chih Wo Sun 白汁蒿筍)

Ingredients:

12	pieces water bamboo-shoots (using heart only)
¼	cup lard
2	teaspoonfuls flour
1	teaspoonful salt
1	slice ham (cooked and minced)
½	cup meat stock

Method:

Boil the water bamboo-shoots in cold water for half an hour. Turn out on to a dish.

To make the sauce, put the lard in a hot frying-pan.

Add the flour and salt, and fry for a second. Then add the meat stock.

Pour this sauce over the water bamboo-shoots in the dish and garnish with ham before serving.

FRIED GREEN BEAN SPROUTS

Ch'ao Tou Ya Ts'ai 炒豆芽菜)

1   lb. bean sprouts
1   large stalk celery (shredded using heart only)
6   mushrooms (soaked and shredded)
1   teaspoonful salt
4   teaspoonfuls soya sauce
½   teaspoonful cornflour
½   cup lard
¼   cup stock

Method:

Heat the lard in a frying-pan, add mushrooms and celery, and fry a little.

Then add the sprouts, salt, soya sauce and stock, and cook for 3 minutes.

Now add the cornflour mixed with a little cold water, stir into the vegetable and serve.

HOME-MADE PICKLES
(P'ao Ts'ai 泡菜)

Ingredients:

- 2   Cucumbers (remove seeds)
- 1   large cauliflower (in coarse pieces)
- ½   foreign cabbage (in coarse pieces)
- 6   green peppers (remove seeds and cut into squares)
- 3   red chilis (remove seeds and cut into squares)
- 1   red carrot (remove skin and cut into squares)
- 2   cups white vinegar
- ½   cup sugar
- 1   teaspoonful salt

Method:

Boil the cauliflower in a deep saucepan for 10 minutes, then add all the above ingredients except the vinegar, sugar and salt.

Now boil the vinegar and pour on to the vegetables, and allow them to soak for 20 minutes.

Turn the vegetables over and cover the saucepan with the lid.

Pickle for 5 hours.   Serve cold.

FRIED SPINACH WITH BAMBOO-SHOOTS AND MUSHROOMS

(Ch'ao Po Ts'ai Tung Ku Sun
炒波菜冬菰筍)

Ingredients:

1	lb. spinach
¼	tinned bamboo-shoots (cut into long thin slices)
10	soaked and cooked mushrooms (cut into long thin slices)
1½	teaspoonfuls salt
½	cup lard
¼	cup stock

Method:

Heat the lard in a frying-pan: add the salt and spinach, and fry for 2 mins.

Then put in the rest of the ingredients, and fry all together for about 4 minutes.

BRAISED GREEN PEAS
(Hui Wan Tou 燴莞豆)

Ingredients:

1	tin of peas
1	bamboo-shoot (cut into small squares)
8	small soaked and cooked mushrooms (cut into small squares)
2	slices Chinese ham (cut into small squares)
1	teaspoonful salt
1½	teaspoonfuls cornflour
1/3	cup lard
1	cup stock

Method:

Heat the lard in a hot frying-pan: add the bamboo-shoot, mushrooms, peas, ham, salt and stock.

Mix the cornflour with a little cold water in a cup and add it slowly to thicken. Cook for about 5 minutes.

SOUPS

(T'ang Lei 湯類)

MELON SOUP

(Tung Kua Chung 多 瓜 盅)

Ingredients:

- ¼ lb. meat fillet
- 2 mushrooms (diced)
- ¼ lb. lotus-seed
- ¼ lb. cooked ham
- 1 stock Chinese onion
- 1 slice of ginger
- 2 teaspoonfuls salt
- 1 teaspoonful wine
- 1 tablespoonful lard
- 4 cups of meat stock

Fry above ingredients together for 2 min.

Method:

Cut melon into halves like a bowl, remove the
seeds and spongy material from the melon.
Cook it in cold water, bring to a boil. Then
remove it standing in a deep bowl. Put
all the cooked ingredients into the melons,
steam for 3 hours.

DUCK'S TONGUE SOUP

(Ya Shê T'ang 鴨舌湯)

Ingredients:

  24   ducks' tongues
  1   small piece ginger
  1   small Chinese onion
  1½ teaspoonfuls salt
  1   teaspoonful Chinese wine
  4   cups meat stock

Method:

Steam the ducks' tongues with the ginger,
   onion, wine, and ½ teaspoonful of salt for
   1 hour.

Bring the meat stock to the boil in a deep
   saucepan. Add all the ingredients and
   another teaspoonful of salt.

Serve in a deep bowl.

MUSHROOM SOUP

(Ch'ing Tun Hua Ku T'ang 清燉花菰湯)

Ingredients:

1/4	lb. mushrooms (soaked)
1/2	chicken
2 1/2	teaspoonfuls salt
6	cups water
1	thin slice ginger
1	stalk Chinese onion
1	teaspoonful wine

Method:

Chop the chicken into large-sized pieces with the bone, then boil it in the water for 3 hours over a slow fire together with the other ingredients.

When serving, use the soup and mushrooms only.

BUTTON MUSHROOM BEAN CURD SOUP

(K'ou Mo Tou Fu T'ang 口蘑豆腐湯)

Ingredients:

- 10 dried mushrooms (K'ou Mo)
- ¼ lb. bean curd (cut into squares)
- 1 teaspoonful salt
- 4 cups stock

Method:

Soak the mushrooms in boiling water for 10
minutes. Take them out and wash them
in cold water 2 or 3 times. Then return
the mushrooms to the original water in
which they had been soaked.

Bring the stock to the boil in a frying pan.

Add the salt, bean curd and the mushrooms
with their water, and bring to the boil a
second time before serving.

CHICKEN AND CUCUMBER SOUP

(Huang Kua Ch'uan Chi T'ang
黃 瓜 川 鷄 湯)

Ingredients:

1	chicken (with bone)
4	cups cold water
1	teaspoonful salt
½	cucumber (sliced)
½	teaspoonful cornflour

Method:

Boil the whole chicken (except the breast) in 4 cups of water for 2 hours to make the soup.

Slice the chicken breast, and mix it thoroughly with ½ teaspoonful of salt, and the cornflour.

When the soup is ready, drain it off, and using only the clear soup, pour it into a frying pan, and boil. When boiling, add the cucumber, chicken breast, and ½ teaspoonful of salt.

Serve at once.

STEAMED TIENTSIN CABBAGE SOUP

(Chêng Pai Ts'ai Tuan 蒸天津白菜叚)

Ingredients:

2 large cabbage hearts (cut into big pieces)
1 slice ham (finely chopped)
1 teaspoonful salt
1 teaspoonful cornflour
1½ cups stock

Method:

Place the cabbage in a deep dish, and steam in a steam cooker for 15 minutes.

Make some sauce in a frying pan with the stock by adding salt, and thickening with the cornflour. Pour this over the cabbage, and garnish with the finely chopped ham.

CHICKEN, MUSHROOM & BAMBOO SHOOT SOUP

(San Hsien T'ang 三鮮湯)

Ingredients:

1   chicken boiled in 6 cups of water for
    1½ hours to make soup
2   breasts of chicken (sliced)
8   fresh mushrooms
1   large bamboo-shoot (sliced)
1   teaspoonful salt
1   teaspoonful wine

Method:

Through a fine strainer strain the chicken
    soup into a hot frying-pan. Bring to the
    boil, then add the chicken breast, fresh
    mushrooms, bamboo shoot, salt and wine.
Bring to the boil again, and serve in a deep
    bowl.

CLEAR DUCK SOUP

(Ch'ing Cheng Ya Tzu T'ang 青蒸鴨子湯)

Ingredients:

1	duck (about 3 lbs.)
1	piece Chinese onion
1	piece ginger
2	slices cooked ham
½	bamboo-shoots
4	big soaked mushrooms (Tung Ku)
1	heaped teaspoonful salt
4	cups water

Method:

Put the whole duck and all the other ingredients in a big bowl. Steam in a double boiler for 2 hours over a moderate fire. Serve in a soup bowl.

DESSERTS

"EIGHT PRECIOUS" RICE PUDDING

(Pa Pao Fan 八寶飯)

Ingredients:

- 2   cups glutinous rice (糯米)
- 4   cups cold water
- 1   cup sugar
- ½   lb. Chinese dates (cooked for 30 mins. and mashed)
- 2   ozs. dried red plums (紅梅)
- 2   ozs. dried green plums (青梅)
- 2   ozs. candied lotus seeds (蓮子)
- 2   ozs. honey dates (蜜棗)
- 2   ozs. chestnuts (cooked and shelled)
- 1   teaspoonful lard.

Method:

Wash the rice three or four times in cold water: Put the washed rice and 4 cups of cold water in a deep saucepan, then boil it for about 5 minutes, and allow to simmer for 20 minutes. Now add the sugar, and stir well.

Now line a 7-inch deep bowl with a piece of
white paper cut into a round shape and
smeared with lard on both sides. Place
the red plums in the centre of the bowl:
then around this, in order, arrange the
green plums, the lotus seeds, the dates,
and, on the outermost edge, the chestnuts.
Now divide the rice into two equal portions: Place one portion over the dried
fruit in the bowl. Cover this with a layer
composed of the mashed dates, and, finally,
place the other portion of rice on top of the
dates. Place the bowl and its contents in
a steamer, and steam for 20 minutes.

Turn out on to dish: remove the paper and
pour the sauce over the pudding before
serving.

For the sauce you need:

½   cup sugar
1   teaspoonful cornflour
1   cup cold water

Method:

Boil the water and sugar in a saucepan, then
mix the cornflour with a little cold water
and add it slowly to the syrup.

ALMOND TEA

(Hsing Jen Ch'a 杏仁茶)

Ingredients:

- ¾ cup uncooked rice soaked in cold water for 15 mins
- ½ cup sweet almonds blanched in boiling water for 15 mins
- ¼ cup bitter almonds soaked in boiling water for 15 mins
- 6 cups cold water
- 2 cups sugar

Method:

Put the rice and almonds in a mortar, and pound thoroughly adding 1 cup of water slowly.

Strain through a muslin bag, squeezing it well.

Add 5 cups of water, then 2 cups of sugar.

Bring to the boil, then boil gently for 7 mins., stirring all the time.

Serve hot or cold.

ROSE PETAL SYRUP CAKE

(Mei Kuei Kuo Cha 玫瑰煾炸)

Ingredients:

3	egg yolks
1	cup cold water
1	tablespoonful rose sugar (玫瑰糖)
½	cup flour
2	teaspoonfuls sugar

Method:

Mix well together the egg, the flour, 2 teaspoonfuls sugar, and the water. Boil until
it sets, then turn out and allow to cool.

Cut it into strips, 2 inches long and ½ inch
wide.

Sprinkle them with a little corn flour.

Fry these in deep fat until light brown.

Sprinkle the rose sugar over them, and serve
with the following syrup:

For the syrup you require:

4	teaspoonfuls sugar
½	teaspoonful corn flour
1	teaspoonful rose petal syrup (玫瑰糖稀)

1   cup cold water

Method:

Bring the water to the boil in a small deep
   saucepan.
Add the sugar and rose petal syrup.
Mix the corn flour with a little water, and add
   it slowly to thicken the syrup.

ALMOND CURD

(Hsing Jen Tou Fu 杏仁豆腐)

Ingredients:

- ½ cup sweet almonds (blanched in boiling water)
- ½ cup uncooked rice (soaked in cold water)
- ¼ cup bitter almonds (soaked in boiling water)
- 2 strips gelatine
- 1¾ cups sugar
- 6 cups water
- 6 cherries (cut in halves)

Method:

Put the almonds and the rice in a grinder, while grinding add 1 cup of water. Pour the liquid into a muslin bag, and squeeze out the watery portion which should be about one cup, to this add 5 cups of water, then add the gelatine and one cup of sugar. Boil until the gelatine has melted. Pour into a flat dish and allow to set. Cut into fairly large diamond shaped pieces.

Sauce:

Boil 3 cups of water, add remaining sugar,
and boil for a few minutes. When cold,
add to the sliced almond curd and decorate
with the cherries.

WALNUT TEA

(Hê T'ao Jen Ch'a 核桃仁茶)

Ingredients:

   2   cups walnuts (shelled and blanched in
          boiling water for 15 minutes)
   ½   cup uncooked rice (soaked in cold
          water for 15 minutes)
   2   cups sugar
   6   cups water

Method:

Grind the walnuts and rice together thoroughly in a mortar, adding water, a little at a
   time, while grinding.
Then add what remains of 3 cups of water
   to the walnut and rice paste. Squeeze
   through a muslin bag.
To the liquid thus obtained, add 3 more cups
   of water and the sugar, and cook in a deep
   saucepan for 7 mins., stirring all the time.
Serve in cups.

PASTRIES

(Mien Shih 麵食)

揑麵
HOW TO MAKE NOODLES

Fig. 3

Fig. 1

Fig. 4

Fig. 2

HOW TO MAKE NOODLES

(Kan Mien 捍麵)

Ingredients:

    4   eggs (medium size)

    2½ cups of flour

Method:

Beat eggs slightly, mix well with the flour and knead into a soft dough.

Cover with a damp cloth, and allow it to stand for 10 minutes.

Knead again for 5 minutes, sprinkle with cornflour, then roll out till very thin, about 20 inches wide (see fig. 1) Fold into a number of pleats (see fig. 2) then cut across the pleats finely as you would cut rashers of bacon (see fig. 3) and by lifting the ends in the uppermost pleat, you get the long strands of noodles. (see fig. 4)

To cook, drop the noodles into a saucepan of boiling water and boil for 2 minutes.

Turn them out into a colander, and run cold water through it three times. Squeeze out the water and drain.

These noodles can now be used for Chao Mien or Tang Mien.

FRIED NOODLES

(Chi Ssu Ch'ao Mien 鷄絲炒麵)

Ingredients:

Cooked Noodles

1	lb. bamboo-shoot (shredded)
1/4	lb. breast of chicken (shredded)
3	stalks of Chinese celery (heart only) shredded
6	large mushrooms (soaked and shredded)
1/2	large onion (shredded)
1	cup lard
1 1/2	teaspoonfuls salt
4	teaspoonfuls soya sauce
1	egg made into a thin omelet shredded
1	cup stock

Method:

Heat 1/2 cup of lard in a frying pan, add the noodles, sprinkle 1/2 teaspoonful of salt on them and fry one side until a golden brown. Turn over and repeat the process. Turn noodles out on to a dish.

Add 1/3 cup of lard, and fry onion to a light
brown. Put in mushrooms and all the
other ingredients, together with ½ teaspoonful salt, 4 teaspoonfuls soya sauce, 1
cup of stock, and fry for 3-4 minutes.

Divide the contents of the pan into two equal
portions, leave one half in the pan, pour
in the noodles, and mix together, then
replace the other half on this mixture.
Garnish with shredded ham and omelet.

Serve on a large dish while very hot.

Sufficient for 8 persons.

NOODLES IN CHICKEN SOUP

(Chi Ssu T'ang Mien 鷄絲湯麵)

Ingredients:

Noodles +

1 chicken (for making soup)
2 pieces chicken fillet (shredded)
2 bamboo-shoots (shredded)
4 mushrooms (soaked and shredded)
1 bowl green cooked vegetables (any kind)
1 teaspoonful soya sauce
1½ teaspoonfuls salt
⅛ cup lard

Method:

Drop the noodles into boiling water, bring
to a boil. Remove them, and put them
into the chicken soup, which should be
boiling hot, adding 1 teaspoonful salt.
Turn out into a big bowl, or serve the
noodles in individual small bowls.

Heat the lard in a frying pan. Fry chicken
fillet a little, then add bamboo-shoot, mushrooms, vegetables, soya sauce, and ½
teaspoonful salt, and fry together for 3
minutes. Turn out on top of the noodles
in the bowl, or on top of each small bowl.

STEAMED DUMPLINGS

(T'ang Mien Chiao Tzu 燙麵餃子)

Ingredients:

- 2 cups flour
- 1 cup boiling water
- ¼ cup lard
- 12 mushrooms (diced)
- 10 water-chestnuts (diced)
- 1 bamboo-shoot (diced)
- ½ lb. pork (minced)
- 1 teaspoonful sesamum oil
- 1 teaspoonful salt
- 5 teaspoonfuls soya sauce
- 2 teaspoonfuls sugar
- 1 tiny piece Chinese onion (finely chopped)
- 1 tiny slice ginger (finely chopped)
- 1 teaspoonful wine
- 1 teaspoonful cornflour.

Method:

(1) To make filling.

Heat the lard in frying-pan. Fry the pork together with the mushrooms, water chestnuts, bamboo-shoot, onion, ginger,

and sesamum oil. Then add the soya
sauce, sugar and salt. Mix the cornflour with the cold water in a cup and
pour over the pork, stir well, and turn
out into a bowl.

(2) To make wrapping.

Mix the flour with boiling water until it
forms a soft dough. Knead well,
sprinkle with dry flour, and roll into a
long sausage. Pinch off small pieces of
uniform size, and with a small rolling-
pin roll each piece out into a circular
shape about 3 inches in diameter, taking
care to leave the centre thicker than the
edge.

Place on the middle of each circular
piece of dough about one teaspoonful of
the filling mixture. Fold over to make
a semicircle, then press the opposite
edges together with the fingers, and you
have your Chiao Tzu.

When all the Chiao Tzu are made, place
them on a piece of damp cloth in a
steam cage, and steam for about ten
minutes.

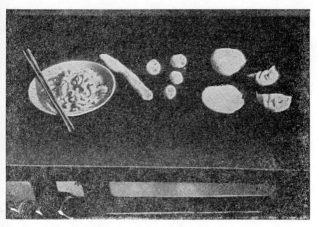

FRIED DUMPLING
(Kuo Teih Chiao Tzu 煱貼餃子)

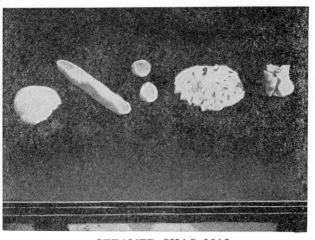

STEAMED SHAO MAI
(Cheng Shao Mai 蒸燒饅)

FRIED DUMPLINGS

(Kuo Tieh Chiao Tzu 焗貼餃子)

¾	lb. pork (minced)
a	little Chinese onion (chopped finely)
a	little ginger (,, ,,)
½	cup lard
1	teaspoonful salt
3	teaspoonfuls soya sauce
2	teaspoonfuls sesamum oil
30	teaspoonfuls cold water

Method:

To the pork add the onion, ginger, salt, soya sauce and sesamum oil, and mix thoroughly together with a pair of chopsticks.

To make Wrapping:

Mix 2 cups of flour with one cup of cold water and knead into a soft dough. Cover with a damp cloth, and allow to stand for 15 minutes before using.

Roll out the dough on a board into a long sausage, then pinch off pieces about the size of a walnut.

Sprinkle flour on each one, and with a small rolling-pin roll it into a thin pancake about

3 inches in diameter. Into each of these pieces put one teaspoonful of the filling mixture. Fold the pancake over, and pinch the edges together with the fingers. To make the fried dumplings put the lard in a frying-pan, arrange the dumplings in rows in the pan, and fry the bottom to a light brown. Now pour ½ cup cold water over them. Cover with a lid, and continue cooking until the water has dried up.

STEAMED SHAO MAI

(Cheng Shao Mai 蒸燒饅)

Ingredients:

1	lb. Pork (minced)
1	small slice ginger (finely chopped)
1	small stalk Chinese onion (,, ,,)
6	mushrooms (soaked and finely chopped)
1	teaspoonful sesamum oil
½	teaspoonful salt
3	teaspoonfuls soya sauce
⅛	teaspoonful sugar
4½	tablespoonfuls cold water

Mix the above ingredients together thoroughly, and leave in a bowl for use as filling.

To make wrapping:

Mix 2 cups of flour with one cup of boiling water until it forms a soft dough. Knead well, and roll into a long sausage, then pinch off pieces of uniform size. With a small rolling pin roll each of these into flat cakes about 3 inches in diameter, leaving the centre thicker than the edge.

Fray the edge of each by first sprinkling flour
over it, and scraping with the lip of a bowl.

Method:

Put about 2 teaspoonfuls of the filling mixture on the centre of each wrapper.
Manipulate the wrapping dough so that it
closes around the filling material, leaving
the edge free, and you have your Shao Mai.

Repeat the process until the filling is used up.

Steam the Shao Mai in a steam cage or double
boiler for 15 minutes.

SPRING ROLLS

(Cha Ch'un Ch'uan 炸春捲)

Ingredients:

¼	lb. breast of chicken (shredded)
4	mushrooms (shredded)
½	onion (shredded)
1	bamboo shoot (shredded)
2	cups bean sprouts
2	cups spinach in 1 inch lengths
1	teaspoonful cornflour
2	teaspoonfuls soya sauce
1	teaspoonful Chinese wine
¼	teaspoonful salt
½	cup lard
¼	cup stock

Method:

Add the salt and ½ teaspoonful cornflour to the chicken and mix well. Put ¼ cup of lard in a pan. When hot, fry the onion just a little. Add the mushrooms, bamboo-shoot, bean sprouts, spinach, and 1 teaspoonful soya sauce, and fry together for 3 minutes. Turn out on to a plate. Place

a little more lard in the pan, then fry the
chicken meat with 1 teaspoonful of wine,
and 1 teaspoonful of soya sauce.   Mix
well, then add the other ingredients with
$\frac{1}{2}$ teaspoonful cornflour stirred with stock
or water.

The above is to be used as filling.

Wrapping for spring rolls:

Take 2 cups of flour, add cold water gradu-
ally and mix until the resulting dough is
of the consistency of marsh-mallow, then
let it stand for 10 minutes before using.
Take the mass in your hand, and by pres-
sing it against a warm greasy frying pan
with a flat surface, a thin sheet is left on
it which resembles a sheet of rice-paper,
about the size of the palm of the hand.
Repeat the process until all the dough is
used up.   Into each piece put 2 teaspoonfuls of the above filling.

Roll up lengthwise and seal the ends with
cold water.   Fry in deep fat till a golden
brown.

SPRING ROLLS
(Cha Ch'um Ch'uan 炸春捲)

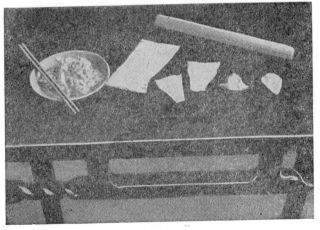

RAVIOLI
(Hum T'um 餛飩)

RAVIOLI

(Hun T'un 餛飩)

Ingredients: for filling.

1/2	lb. chicken (minced)
1	small onion (finely chopped)
1	thin slice ginger („ „)
1	teaspoonful salt
1	teaspoonful soya sauce
1	teaspoonful sesamum oil
1	teaspoonful Chinese wine

Mix the above ingredients thoroughly in a bowl.

Ingredients: for wrapping.

1	cup flour
2	eggs (small size)

Method:

Mix the ingredients well and knead into a dough.   Sprinkle cornflour on rolling board, roll out till very thin about 20 inches wide, and then cut into strips about 2½ inches in width.   Place the strips one on top of the other, and cut them up into "isosceles trapezoids" thus:

On to each of these pieces of dough, place half teaspoonful of the filling towards the shorter side (S). Turn this side over the filling and roll halfway up towards the longer side (L). Double this over on itself, and pinch the ends of the rolled up portion together, leaving the longer side free. The filling should be sufficient for 50 to 60 ravioli. Fry in deep fat until a golden brown.

PANCAKE ROLLS

(Ho Yeh Ping 荷葉餅)

Ingredients for making the Pancakes:

    2   cups flour
    ¼   cup lard
    1   cup boiling water.

Method:

Mix the flour with boiling water and knead
into a soft dough. Shape the dough into
a long sausage, then pinch off small pieces
of uniform size. Roll each of these between the palms of your hands, and press
it flat. Take two of these and brush a little
lard between them, and roll them out
5 inches in diameter. Fry them on both
sides in a dry flat pan, then tear them apart,
and they are ready for serving.

Ingredients for Filling:

    ½   lb. chicken (shredded)
    1½ lb. bean sprouts
    1   stalk celery (shredded)
    3   soaked mushrooms (shredded)

½   foreign onion (shredded)
1   teaspoonful salt.
3   teaspoonfuls soya sauce
½   teaspoonful sugar
1/3 cup lard
½   teaspoonful cornflour.

Method:

Heat ¼ cup of the lard in a frying-pan. Brown the onion and add the bean sprouts, celery, mushrooms and the salt. Allow to cook for 2 mins, finally add the sugar and 4 teaspoonfuls of soya sauce. Turn out into a dish.

Mix chicken with cornflour and salt thoroughly. Put the rest of the lard in the pan. Fry the chicken and add 1 teaspoonful of soya sauce. Replace the bean sprouts mixture in the pan. Fry for 2 mins. Serve with the pancakes.

Suggested Menus

(1)

Fried Rice

Fried Beef Fillet

Roast Crisp Duck

Red Sauce Rump Pork

Braised Shrimps

Fried Mustard Greens

Steamed Tientsin Cabbage Soup

(2)

Fried Noodles

Roast Stuffed Chicken

Egg and Beef Omelet

Brown Sauce Mandarin Fish

Fried Spinach with Bamboo Shoot and

Mushrooms

Velvet Chicken with Corn

(3)

Fried Dumplings
Minced Pigeon
Stuffed Green Peppers
Fried Fish Cakes
Stewed Rice Flour Pork
Tientsin Cabbage with Chestnuts
Melon Soup
Served with Rice

(4)

Spring Rolls
Sweet and Sour Pork
Fried Chicken with Pepper and Brown Sauce
Smoked Fish
Stewed Meat Balls with Shantung Cabbage
Braised Green Peas
Duck's Tongue Soup
Served with Rice

(5)

Fried Ravioli (Hun Tun)
Walnut Chicken
Fried Minced Fish
Brown Sauce Beef
Velvet Chicken (Imitation)
Braised Fresh Mushrooms with Chinese
Cabbage
Chicken and Cucumber Soup
Served with Rice

(6)

Noodles In Chicken Soup
Red Sauce Duck
White Sauce Fish (sour)
Fried Duck Liver
Roast Shaslick Pork
Stuffed Mushrooms
Home Made Pickles
Served with Rice

(7)

Pancake Rolls

Fried Shrimp Balls

Fried Green Bean Sprouts

Pineapple Ginger and Duck

Stewed Pork with Bamboo Shoot

Mushroom Soup (Hua Ku)

Almond Tea

(8)

Roast Stuffed Chicken

Gold Coin Chicken

Fried Fish with Red Sauce

Stewed Shin of Beef

Steamed Dumplings (Chiao Tzu)

White Sauce Water Bamboo Shoots

Chicken, Mushroom and Bamboo Shoot Soup

(9)

Stewed Chicken Chestnut
Steamed Shao Mai
Crab Fat with Green Vegetables
Stewed Pork with Bamboo Shoot
Foreign Cabbage
Served with Rice
Walnut Tea

(10)

Steamed Dumplings
Chili Oil Chicken and Spinach
Fried Shrimp Cakes
Crab Omelet
Roast Chicken (boneless)
Fried Wild Duck
Braised Bamboo Shoots
Clear Duck Soup
Served with Rice
Rose Petal Syrup Cakes

MEANING	PICTOGRAPH	CHARACTER	PRONUNCIATION
Saltish			Hsien
Sweet			Tien
Sour			Suan
Bitter			K'u
Acrid			La
Fragrant			Hsiang

Chinese Characters for Different Tastes

INDEX FOR CHINESE WORDS

INDEX